Letting Go Without Losing Control

Control

■

JOHN AND SHIRLEY PAYNE

*the Institute
of Management*

PITMAN PUBLISHING

The Insitute of Management (IM) is at the forefront of management development and best management practice. The Institute embraces all levels of management from students to chief executives. It provides a unique portfolio of services for all managers, enabling them to develop skills and achieve management excellence. If you would like to hear more about the benefits of membership, please write to Department P, Institute of Management, Cottingham Road, Corby NN17 1TT. This series is commissioned by the Institute of Management Foundation.

Pitman Publishing
128 Long Acre, London WC2E 9AN

A Division of Longman Group UK Limited

First published in Great Britain 1994

© John & Shirley Payne 1994

British Library Cataloguing in Publication Data
A CIP catalogue record for this book can be obtained
from the British Library.

ISBN 0 273 60425 2 (Paperback)
ISBN 0 273 60746 4 (Casebound)

Typeset by PanTek Arts, Maidstone
Printed and bound in Great Britain
by Bell and Bain Ltd, Glasgow.

The Publisher's policy is to use paper manufactured from sustainable forests.

Contents

■

A VOTE OF THANKS

We would like to thank all those people (too numerous to mention individually) who have given us ideas, and tales of good and bad delegation over a lot of years.

Thanks also to David Crosby of Pitman who has provided help and advice from the original idea for this book through to its publication.

Finally, thanks to you for buying it. We hope you enjoy it and gain from it.

Introduction

The scene is a multi-storey factory. There is David, a brand new manager who was previously a Section Leader within the department he now manages. Once David knew he was to be promoted, he promoted one of the members of his section, Karen, to his old role as Section Leader. It is Day One and David is sitting there thinking, *Okay, I've got an office, my own secretary and a brand new car – now what? I had better nip down to the stores and just see how Karen is coping with the new role.* So off he goes to the stores to see Karen. After a couple of hours lending Karen a helping hand, David returns to his office thinking, *Showed a bit of interest and didn't just abdicate and leave her on her own. That's a good enough start.* He pours himself a well-earned cup of coffee and notices a phone message on his desk.

> *David, please come and see me when you get back.*
>
> *Thanks.*
>
> *Paul (Managing Director)*

David surmises on the way to Paul's office *That's a nice thought. I expect he wants to give me the corporate pat on the back and a welcome to the management type speech. Might even get lunch.*

'Ah Morning, David. How are things going in the new role?'

'Fine, Paul. I spent a bit of time with Karen this morning just to make sure she was happy'.

'David, what is the situation with the strike on the third floor?'. . . . Long shocked pause.

'Er, um, sorry Paul, I didn't know there was one. I'll check and be back in a couple of minutes.'

David now becomes a contender for the Olympics by rushing up to the third floor taking three steps at a time. He pauses outside the door, panting rather heavily by now and thinks *Don't panic. Get your breath back and walk in calmly.* After a minute's pause to let the rate fall from cardiac arrest level, in he goes . . . and . . . NOTHING!

Everything seems absolutely normal. After a couple of subtle questions to the charge-hand, David thinks that he might have misheard so better check all the floors . . . again . . . NOTHING!

So back to Paul's office goes David feeling more than a little puzzled.

2

'Paul, you asked about the third floor strike. I'm sorry but there's no sign of any strike on the third floor or anywhere else for that matter.'

'I know, David!' came the curt reply from Paul. *'There never WAS a strike, but you didn't know that without checking, did you? This will seem hard on your first day but you must remember that you are managing a department now so you must be aware of what is going on throughout the WHOLE factory, not just in the bit you used to control. You promoted Karen because she can do your old job. She knows where your office is, you know. Let her get on with it whilst you look at the broader picture.'*

David left feeling he had learned a hard but important lesson!*That wasn't the kind of initiation into management I'd expected but he's right, damn it. I wasn't where I should be, or doing what I should be doing. I didn't want to abdicate but I didn't want to lose control either, and what makes it worse is Karen probably thought I was guilty of well-intended interference. This delegation business is going to be hard, but I've made a start.'*

Just like driving, nobody wants to admit to being a bad delegator!

What will this book do for you?

Most managers find it hard to 'let go', i.e. delegate, and there is often an underlying (and natural) concern about losing control.

This book should help you to review how you see DELEGATION now, compare how you do it with some practical principles, and develop or enhance your skills in this important but very difficult area. There are few 'absolutes' in management so you should view the principles contained in this book as guidelines. Situations and people differ widely, so these guidelines will not apply equally to every delegation opportunity that you face. See them as areas for consideration. Only you can decide when, and to what extent, each applies. We hope that as a result of reading this book, you identify some ideas which will help you to delegate more effectively **without losing control.**

What are the objectives for this book?

When you have read this book, you should know:

- the difference between delegating and assigning work
- the common traps when trying to delegate and know how to avoid them
- what can and can't be delegated
- how to choose someone to do the task(s)
- how to prepare for and run the delegation discussion
- how to keep control without interfering
- what to do if things go wrong.

The style and structure of the book.

We are very strong believers in practical training and use a 'learning by doing' approach on our training courses. Consequently, we have tried to make this book as interactive as possible, and actively encourage your input to help you gain most from reading it.

Where possible, we have included 'Activity' sections that will help you to assess your own views and approach so that you can compare your way with the ideas suggested in the book.

The Activity sections are marked with a symbol:

Whilst it is not essential to complete these sections, we believe that you will gain far more from the book if you do try them.

Each chapter covers a specific aspect of delegation. Each starts with objectives and an outline of what is covered there.

There are examples of good and bad delegation throughout the book. Some have come from the authors' own experiences, and some are from others (course attendees, managers, friends, etc.). All names (organisations and individuals) have been changed to protect the guilty (including us!!!).

At the end of each chapter there is a summary or checklist to remind you of the key points, together with a section for you to record the points that struck home for you.

How you might use this book.

You might have bought this book for one of two main reasons:

'I'm new and want to learn how to delegate.'

You might be aiming towards a management job (or have recently taken up your first management post), realise that good delegation is an important (or vital) skill for a manager, possibly not know too much about actually delegating, and want to learn how to delegate as effectively as possible. You may not have delegated before but that does not mean you know nothing! You may well have been on the receiving end of delegation and so will know something about it.

The best way of using the book is probably to work through it and complete all of the Activity sections where your input is requested. In other words, use it as a workbook.

'I'm experienced but I want some tips on delegation.'

You might be an experienced manager who knows how hard it is to delegate well, want to compare your own approach with that suggested in the book and identify your own strengths and weaknesses, and enhance your skills in this area. It is important to remember to be honest about your own strengths and weaknesses. Often, people are quite happy to try to improve their weaknesses but can often forget (or ignore) their strengths. We believe that it is *as important* to build on strengths as it is to correct weaknesses.

The best way of using the book is probably to read through Chapters 1 and 2 which cover the basics to compare your view of delegation with ours, complete the self-assessment section at the end of

Chapter 2 that will indicate the areas of delegation on which you might want to concentrate, and then read only those chapters or sections which apply to your requirements. Having proposed selective reading (to save busy people some time), there is nothing to stop you reading the whole thing of course.

2

Do you really 'let go'?

Overview of this chapter

This is *your* chapter. The idea is to help you to review your understanding of delegation and identify your strengths and weaknesses with regard to this skill.

You do not *have* to complete this section but we think it highly desirable. If you are trying to get somewhere, it's important to know where you are now. That way, at least you know how far you will have to travel!

What are the objectives for this chapter?

When you have read this chapter, you should:

■ know your strengths and weaknesses with regard to delegating

■ have clearly identified the results that you want from reading this book.

What is covered in this chapter?

■ What does 'delegation' mean to you?

■ How good a delegator are you now?

■ Getting other people's opinions to help you.

■ Identifying your strengths and weaknesses, and the results you want from reading this book.

What does 'delegation' mean to you?

Delegation seems to be one of those words that mean all things to all people. Please take a few minutes to note down your thoughts below:

_____

_____

_____

How good a delegator are you now?

What follows is a fairly typical situation that requires delegation. No single situation is likely to cover every aspect of delegation but we hope that this example will enable you to broadly think through how you would actually approach delegation.

WHAT DO YOU NEED TO DO?

■ Read through the situation, and decide how you would probably handle it.

■ Note your ideas down in the section that follows the situation.

■ After this, we have listed the factors that we consider to be important in this situation. (We know it is tempting, but **DON'T CHEAT**.)

■ You will then be able to complete a checklist that will compare your approach with these factors.

THE SITUATION

You are the Training Manager in an engineering firm of 800 people and have a team of five people reporting to you – one Management/ Supervisory Trainer, one clerical/computer trainer, two technical trainers, and a secretary (who also types the course material for the trainers).

Today is Tuesday and a Departmental Meeting has previously been arranged for Monday of next week. The objective of the meeting is to agree the training plans and budget for next year with the Personnel Director. All your trainers have already produced individual training plans and you have produced a budget. Your management trainer currently manages the departmental budget very effectively for you and this will continue.

You have just been asked by the parent company in the USA to attend a training meeting in New York next Monday to explain your innovative approach to technical training which has impressed them. You will fly out on Saturday, fly back on Tuesday, and return to the office on Wednesday. The Personnel Director (to whom you report) is more than happy about this and feels that it is important to help them. However, she wants the departmental meeting to go ahead anyway as the budget must be agreed on that day to fit into the company financial planning timetable.

You cannot be in two places at once so you intend to delegate the task of running the departmental meeting to your management trainer. He often acts as your deputy to cover your absences and has run two successful departmental meetings for you before. However, this is a very important meeting as it concerns next year's training plan and budget. The presence of the Personnel Director will make it rather more daunting than usual, especially as she is a powerful lady prone to take over in meetings. You know how to cope with this without giving offence.

You are in the office for the rest of this week. Your management trainer has no courses this week and is trying to catch up with some administrative work (writing some course material, follow-up phone calls to previous course delegates, monthly training report, etc.).

9

HOW WOULD YOU, AS THE TRAINING MANAGER, HANDLE THE SITUATION?

THE FACTORS THAT WE CONSIDER TO BE IMPORTANT IN THIS SITUATION

We have simply listed relevant factors here. Their importance and how they are actually used will be covered in later sections of the book.

Before the discussion

Objective Decide the result you expect the management trainer to achieve at the meeting

Background Why must the meeting take place, why choose the management trainer to run it, how might he feel about being asked?

Experience Decide on the management trainer's experience, strengths (prior meetings, budgets), and 'weaknesses' (handling the Director).

During the discussion

Throughout the meeting it is important that you show trust and confidence in the management trainer's ability to handle the meeting. If YOU don't sound as if you believe he can do it, then why should HE believe he can.

Rapport Put him at ease, establish rapport.

Purpose Explain the situation, why the meeting must go ahead as planned, and why you have chosen the management trainer to run it.

Rather than give YOUR views, it is important to ask the management trainer for HIS views on:

Workload Current workload, and ensure preparation is feasible.

Knowledge What he needs to know. Although he runs the current budget, he may need to know how you have arrived at the budget for next year. The same may apply to the composite training plan. He may also need to know the criteria by which the Director would judge the training plan/budget.

Plan What he needs to prepare, what he would see as a specific, result-oriented objective for the meeting, and how he would run it. Correct this plan only if there is a basic flaw. You should let him do it his way.

Potential Difficulties Any potential difficulties he might foresee, e.g. a take-over by the Personnel Director, rejection of the training plan or budget, and how he would prevent/deal with them. Again, modify only if there is a basic flaw. He may ask you to take action, e.g. a word with the Director before you go.

Controls For commitment, it is important to let the trainer suggest when you should meet, and what is required from you at the meeting(s). He would probably suggest a meeting after preparation but before the weekend.

Authority What authority he needs. Give authority to make modifications to the plan/budget (within certain limits) to achieve the agreement of the Director. It may also help him if you notify the team that he will run the meeting and has your authority to make the necessary decisions in the meeting.

Feelings How he actually *feels* now about running the meeting, deal with any concerns he may have, and check he is prepared to take it on. Look for 'commitment' rather than just 'acceptance'.

'Lifeline' To avoid unnecessary interference, offer the opportunity for them to come and discuss any concerns during preparation.

Follow-up Explain you would like to hear the outcome and discuss how the meeting went after your return. Jointly agree the date.

Summary Summarise the result expected from the meeting, key actions and dates/times.

After the discussion

Follow-up meeting Thank him for handling it for you. Review the outcome of the departmental meeting, discuss what went well and what could have been improved. Agree any necessary actions. Check how he feels having done it.

CHECKLIST FOR COMPARISON

Decide, from your handling of the situation, to what extent you considered the factors we have listed, and make whatever notes you think are helpful.

Questions to consider:

Overall, did you delegate, abdicate, or over-control?

_____

_____

11

Did you **involve** them , or **tell** them how to do it?

_____

_____

Did you give them **authority** as well as responsibility?

_____

_____

Did you let them set the controls, i.e. when to meet you?

_____

_____

Did you actually check how they **felt**?

_____

_____

Did you check for **commitment** versus **acceptance**?

_____

_____

Did you **summarise** at the end?

_____

_____

Did you plan a follow-up meeting?

_____

_____

Look back at the factors we identified. Were there any major areas that you missed. If so, why was that?

_____

_____

How did you do?

Getting other people's opinions to help you

Now for the really tough part. You can only try this if you delegate already. The idea is to ask people whose opinion you trust, how they view your approach to delegation. 'Aaaaaagh! I'm not that much of a masochist', could be your reaction. There are risks of course and only you can decide whether the pay-off is worth the risk. So let's look at both sides of the coin.

THE BENEFITS

- You find out how the person on the receiving end actually *feels* about your approach to delegation. Their ideas should help you to make your delegation discussions even more effective.

- There is no one guaranteed right way that suits everyone and every situation, so the information you gain should help you to tailor the discussion to suit the individual/situation.

- Asking your own manager could well provide a useful view from outside. This is only really viable if they are reasonably close to the action; a manager based in a different building may find this diffi-cult or even impossible. However they may still be able to give general impressions if not any detail.

- Asking your secretary/P.A. can be really useful. They are often on the receiving end of a considerable amount of 'unconscious' delegation. Asking them for their views should provide the benefits mentioned above but, additionally, may significantly improve day-to-day organi-sation that is so often just written off as office routine. The discussion may well provide more delegation opportunities.

13

THE RISKS

- Worst case: someone tells you that you don't delegate at all or that you delegate badly. So from here on it can only improve! The real problem we have got is coping with our own ego. No-one likes criti-cism but you did ask them because you trust their opinion and intend to do something with it. If you accept that what they are saying is true then involving them in improving matters is a big step forward.

- Someone unjustly criticises your attempts at delegation and the discussion turns into an argument. This is down to YOU. It can be prevented by a few ground rules. The most important goes some-thing like 'Tell me what you think I do well and why, and what you think I could improve and how. If possible, try to give me examples to illustrate what you are saying'.

This is really asking them for a balanced view, and to give you facts to back up their opinions. If you still feel it is unjust, ask yourself why? Are they factually wrong or is their perception just different to yours?

■ You are not told the whole truth. This might happen when asking someone who reports to you. Few people have a death-wish! Explaining, at the start of the discussion, why you are looking at the way you delegate and why you are asking *them* for their views should help. You might also try asking them how they feel about giving you this sort of feedback, and provide whatever reassurance is needed.

Whatever you do, do *not* confirm their worst fears by 'zapping' them for trying to be honest with you. Have you ever seen a mum or dad in a park with a naughty youngster who rushes off towards the park gate (and the main road) on his own? He hesitantly comes when called back and then GETS A SMACK for, as he sees it, coming back! What would YOU do next time? 'Ah, but adults don't think like toddlers, do they?' you might say. Really?

IDENTIFYING YOUR STRENGTHS AND WEAKNESSES, AND THE RESULTS YOU WANT FROM READING THIS BOOK

Making a few notes on the following questions will help you gain the most from the book.

IDENTIFYING WHAT YOU WANT TO GAIN FROM THIS BOOK

Firstly, based on your work on the foregoing delegation situation and any feedback you have received from others, note down your **strengths** regarding delegation:

_____

_____

_____

_____

_____

Next, based on the same information, note your **weaknesses**:

_____

_____

_____

_____

_____

Now, decide what **results you want** from reading this book. (Try to be as specific as you can). After reading this book, I want to know/be able to:

_____

_____

_____

_____

_____

Finally, if you want to avoid reading the whole book, identify **which chapters** of this book **are most relevant** to the results that you want:

_____

_____

_____

_____

3

Why you should let go

Overview of this chapter

Delegation can mean all things to all people. In this chapter, we will define what it means, clear up a common area of confusion, and review the benefits of delegating effectively.

What are the objectives for this chapter?

When you have read this chapter, you should:

■ know what delegation actually means, and how it differs from assigning normal work
■ know the benefits of delegating effectively.

What is covered in this chapter?

■ What does 'delegation' mean?
■ Delegating versus assigning normal work.
■ The benefits of delegating effectively.

What does 'delegation' mean?

One dictionary definition of 'delegation' is:

'To give duties, powers, etc. to another person as representative'.

This can give the impression that everything comes from the manager with nothing much from the delegatee. 'I'm going to give you a very responsible job. I'll make you responsible for being an idiot and treat you accordingly,' could be a cynical alternative.

To delegate well means involving the delegatee in the process. Our definition is shown here. Now let's take this definition apart bit by bit.

DELEGATION IS:

Entrusting part of your job as a manager to some-one else (usually a team member), together with the responsibility for its achievement, and the authority necessary to carry it out.

'ENTRUSTING'

This is key! Unfortunately, too many managers see it as simply giving a series of instructions and then keeping a tight control over their execution. (Sometimes it is the delegatee who would like to be doing the executing!!!)

Trust is a two-way process. The manager must have, and show, faith in the delegatee's ability to carry out the task effectively. The delegatee must trust the manager's motives in giving him the task to do.

Entrusting does NOT mean abdication. Abdication occurs when a manager attempts to duck 'accountability' for the task.

ACCOUNTABILITY IS:

being ultimately responsible for the work of a unit or department, i.e. *the buck stops here !*

Conversation between Sales Director (Marion) and Sales Manager (Ken):

'Come in, Ken. I have had a disturbing phone call this morning. ABC plc, our largest customer, has just received that proposal from your salesman, John. You know, the one he sent whilst you were away. Verbally he quoted £14,000 for the machine; they said OK. When the proposal arrived, the figure was £17,000 and they had already placed the order on trust...'

'Whoa. It's not MY fault. I can't watch everything, especially when I'm away, you know! I normally sign the ABC proposals but this time I told him to sign the quotation on my behalf. John shouldn't have pulled a stunt like that. Have a go at him not me.'

'Ken, John reports to you as the Sales Manager so the buck stops with YOU. He is responsible for selling ethically and effectively. You are account-

able for the work of your sales team, including anything that they do in your absence with your authority.'

'Remember last month when your team made 200 per cent of target. You run the team so you got the credit even though they did the selling. You must also expect the criticism when things go wrong.

'Sorry, Ken, but you allowed it to happen. Think about why it happened, what you are going to do about the £3,000 difference, and try to prevent any recurrence.'

Ken (the Sales Manager) had delegated to John (the salesman), the responsibility for preparing the ABC quote, and had given him the authority to sign it on Ken's behalf. So far so good! What Ken then attempted to do was to 'pass the buck' and 'delegate' accountability to John as well. Marion (the Sales Director) spotted this and rightly corrected his misconception.

'PART OF *YOUR* JOB AS A MANAGER'

Delegation is often confused with 'assigning work'.

19

Part of a manager's job is to use the resources effectively to achieve the necessary results. This involves dividing up the work and assigning it to the appropriate people. Giving someone a task to do which is part of their normal job is 'assigning work'. By virtue of the role they perform, they already have some responsibilities and, possibly, a certain amount of authority.

Whilst many of the principles involved in assigning work and delegating are similar, delegation involves extra responsibility outside the normal job and, often, extra authority.

Suppose, for example, you are the manager of a computer department. Let's say that you have four programmers reporting to you. A request arrives for a new program. Deciding which of the programmers should write it, and briefing the person, is 'assigning work'. However, the decision as to whether a program should be written internally or a piece of commercial software purchased may normally be taken by the computer manager. If one of the programmers were asked by the manager to make this decision, that would be 'delegating'.

'TO SOMEONE ELSE (USUALLY A TEAM MEMBER)'

The most common form of delegation is between a manager and someone directly reporting to that manager. It is possible to delegate sideways, or at advanced level, upwards!!!

However, a word of warning. If you try this *too* often, your own boss is likely to start questioning the reasons for this, e.g. are *you* prepared to make decisions? Is there no one in your team that you trust? etc.

'WITH THE RESPONSIBILITY FOR ITS ACHIEVEMENT'

'Responsibility' means being answerable for meeting a specific objective, e.g. successfully completing a specific task by a set time/date. Remember that you cannot delegate 'accountability'.

'AND THE AUTHORITY NECESSARY TO CARRY IT OUT'

'Authority', we see as the power to make independent decisions. This means that the person is empowered to make decisions without having to get approval from the delegator. Again, the delegator is still accountable for them.

20

What are the benefits of delegating effectively?

Firstly, what do you think they are?

_____

_____

_____

_____

_____

_____

_____

_____

_____

_____

_____

_____

_____

_____

THE MAIN BENEFITS OF DELEGATING EFFECTIVELY ARE:

- the ability to make more effective use of your own time
- the ability to develop the skills of the members of your team
- the ability to motivate
- the ability to make 'better' decisions

MORE EFFECTIVE USE OF YOUR OWN TIME

Have there ever been enough hours in the day to do everything that you wanted to do? Probably not, very often! It is all too easy to get side-tracked from the vital tasks, to the less important, to the trivial even. In an ideal world, it shouldn't happen, but reality says that it does.

How often have you received a phone call and thought, *That's only a quickie. I'll do that now?* You leave whatever it was you were doing (probably something totally insignificant, like finding an instant cure for the hole in the ozone layer), go to another department only to find that the person you needed to see is somewhere else, and then take an hour to find them and sort it out.

This sort of thing also happens with tasks that could and should be delegated. Some managers spend a disproportionate amount of time doing things that they simply do not *need* to be doing. Consequently, they are not making effective use of their time.

Create a small management 'miracle'.

Delegate more, and make more hours.

Effective delegation will free-up time for the more important tasks for which you are paid. Some people seem to prioritise their work on the basis of how 'urgent' it is rather than on how 'important' it is. Often some of the less important tasks can be delegated, freeing time for you to concentrate on the more important ones. This does not mean giving a team member all the rubbish that you cannot be bothered to do.

21

DEVELOPING THE SKILLS OF YOUR TEAM

Most managers have a responsibility to train and develop the people in their team. If your responsibilities/objectives don't include that, why not? We believe that a key part of any manager's job is to help each team member to receive appropriate training to help them perform to the best of their abilities, and to help them develop to a point where they can progress to the next stage in their career.

Some people do not want promotion, being happy to do what they are doing. Sadly that is seen by some managers as a negative. WE NEED THESE PEOPLE! It is impossible to promote everybody but most people want to be good at what they do.

Part of the delegation process involves some form of coaching. The manager can help the team member learn to do things that he or she may not have been able to do before, and so increase their capabilities.

MOTIVATION

The more someone can do, the more they can be motivated. Good delegation is one of the strongest motivators; bad delegation is one of the strongest demotivators! You can probably think back to examples of both from your own experiences. Do you agree?

Good delegation provides the opportunity for challenge and responsibility, together with recognition and a terrific sense of achievement when the task is completed successfully. Bad delegation causes frustration, a sense of being 'dropped in it' with no help, and feelings of inadequacy. Not very pleasant!

'BETTER' DECISIONS

'Better' compared with what? Compared with rushed decisions, that's what. By freeing up time for the important decisions that you have to make, you should have time to give them adequate consideration.

There is however another side to 'better decisions'. Some people believe that the best decisions are 'made at the coal-face'. In other words, by the person closest to the situation. The more remote the person, the more the decision rests on good information being communicated quickly and accurately.

An example that illustrates this principle in play concerns a private firm that was experiencing cash-flow problems. The story goes that the boss explained to the senior managers that they needed to cut back on expenditure immediately. Several areas of discretionary spend were identified and a decision was made to cut them back in the short term. However they still had a shortfall.

Due to the nature of the firm and its business, travel and accommodation expenses incurred by staff on business was a very large item of expenditure and he felt that potential short-term savings could be made there. The senior managers agreed and decided that a 15 per cent saving on travel and accommodation over a three-month period would be realistic, and that would solve the problem.

How, in your opinion, would this idea actually be implemented? Most people would say something like: only senior managers would approve expenditure; vital trips only would be authorised; cheaper hotels; car sharing; and the departmental managers keeping a tight grip on expenditure. Was that what you put?

Now for the bombshell! Apparently, the boss asked the senior managers to tell their managers to delegate decisions on travel and accommodation as far DOWN the line as they considered appropriate, whilst still being accountable for the outcome, and explain the reasons why this was being done. This meant that, with the approval of the manager, an employee could decide if the trip was necessary and how it would be handled, incur the expense, and claim it back against receipts without argument.

23

Any guess as to the result? Apparently, the saving was 25 per cent in the first month alone (and it continued). So what decisions were being made 'at the coal-face' that were not made before?

People arranged among themselves to share cars rather than make separate trips, use cheap hotels for short stays, travel second class on the train rather than first class, stay with relatives or friends where possible instead of using a hotel, etc.

You might be thinking that the departmental managers should have been doing this sort of thing anyway. Maybe, but how many 'expense systems' would allow you to stay with friends and buy them a meal, instead of staying in a hotel at twice the cost?

Obviously this decision involved a high degree of trust, but it was sensible trust. Remember the managers were told 'to delegate as far down the line as they considered appropriate'. So if there was someone who did not justify that sort of trust, the manager had the option to retain authority. The decision also showed trust in the judgement of the managers.

If the original decision had gone wrong, the boss (as the person accountable for this policy decision) would have had to answer to the other owners of the business.

There are probably only a few people who would have the courage to delegate to that extent in those circumstances but, assuming the story is true, the trust certainly paid off.

We would like to work for that boss. He puts the right value on his people, and deserved the outcome.

SUMMARY – CHAPTER 3

What is delegation?

Entrusting part of your job as a manager to someone else (usually a team member), together with the responsibility for its achievement and the authority necessary to carry it out.

What are the benefits?

- to enable you to make effective use of your own time
- to develop the skills of the members of your team
- to motivate
- 'better' decisions

4

What stops people letting go?

Overview of this chapter

'Most managers do not delegate enough! In this chapter we will look at the reasons for this and what can be done to overcome them.

25

What are the objectives for this chapter?

When you have read this chapter, you should:

■ know the main reasons why some managers feel they do not/cannot delegate sufficiently

■ have decided on the validity of those reasons

■ have identified what can be done to overcome them.

Before we start looking at these reasons, note down your thoughts on two questions:

1 Do you (or managers you know) delegate enough?
2 If not, why do you think that is? List the main factors.

_____

_____

_____

_____

_____

What is covered in this chapter?

The barriers to delegation:

- What if I'm not sure how to delegate properly?
- Won't I lose control?
- It's quicker to do it myself, isn't it?
- I can do it better, can't I?
- But I won't be needed any more.

How senior managers view managers who delegate well, and why.

The barriers to delegation

We know the benefits of delegating effectively. They are powerful, so why is it that some people just don't seem to delegate enough, or even at all?

We spoke to a number of managers at all levels who were honest enough to say that, either they did not delegate at all, or delegated very little. We then asked them why that was.

In the main, there were a multitude of different reasons but some of the reasons came up time and time again. Those reasons are listed above as questions under the heading of 'What is covered in this chapter'. Firstly, compare your thoughts with these reasons. Did you put similar reasons (albeit stated slightly differently)?

What we are now going to do is to look at each of these reasons and decide whether it is a 'reason', or an 'excuse' for not delegating. In our eyes, a reason is a justifiable cause, whereas an excuse *sounds* justifiable, but really is not.

 Before reading any further, look through your earlier list of reasons for not delegating. Be totally honest with yourself and decide whether those you have listed are 'reasons' or 'excuses'. Mark them as 'R' or 'E' if it helps.

What if I'm not sure how to delegate properly?

Anyone who says something like, 'Delegating is easy. I'm good at it', worries us. It is *not* easy to let go and still keep control.

When someone is considering delegating for the first time, it is natural to be concerned about 'doing it properly', (it happens to experienced managers as well!). HOW to do it properly involves knowing and using the principles of effective delegation. That is precisely where this book should help if that is a concern that you have.

Nothing can guarantee 100 per cent success but, if you follow the ideas in this book, you should certainly reduce the likelihood of serious problems.

Some people might say, 'I have never been trained to delegate so how can I be expected to do it properly.' It may be true, but that is an excuse, not a reason! There are those who expect others to do it all for them. To those people we would ask, 'What have *you* done to help yourself?' Courses are valuable but they are not the only means of learning.

In order to learn how to delegate well, we believe that a person needs to have the ability to understand the requirements, the opportunity to practise and apply them (and receive feedback where possible), and, most important of all, they need the right attitude.

People *can* learn to delegate effectively if they really want to do it.

THE IMPORTANCE OF ATTITUDE

If someone does not *want* to learn, it is virtually impossible to teach them anything. Our attitude is probably the one thing over which we have total control. We can *choose* whether we view things positively or negatively. If something bad happens to us, there is no law that says we must view it negatively and carry a chip on our shoulder for the rest of our lives. Now you might be thinking, 'how can you possibly view a negative event positively?'

Let's try an example. Some years ago I was studying for a degree. That particular part of the course required attendance at a one week residential workshop to extend and practise some of the skills covered by the course. Also on the same course was a chap (we will call him 'David' for the sake of the story, and to avoid any embarrassment) who had contracted a serious illness that left him wheelchair-bound, after a previously physically active life. His will to learn new things and his sense of fun were amazing. In fun, he would propel his chair faster than it could be pushed and roar with laughter when the gasping pedestrian (me!) got left behind. He was the first to volunteer to act as a 'guinea pig' or lead a group and, it transpired, had got high grades throughout his degree course. His only problem, according to David, was that he had 'round legs'. He was a source of inspiration to everybody when we were finding things difficult (that was often!) and constantly helped or cheered people up. Everyone would have understood if he had felt 'hard-done-by' or felt he could not cope with some activity or other, but that was most definitely *not* David!

His attitude to learning was the most positive I have ever seen and it just shows what can be done when you believe that you can do it. Getting back to delegation, you can learn if you really want to. An old adage says, 'You are never too old to learn, if you are not too proud to listen!' Attitude again!

27

However, having the right attitude to help you to learn the principles is only part of the requirement. To delegate well means that you must also know the skills and knowledge of the people to whom you might delegate, and understand what is involved in the job that you intend to delegate.

Looking more generally, if someone moves into a new management role with an unfamiliar team, then 'I'm not sure how to do it properly' is probably a valid reason for not delegating much initially. It takes time to get to know the people involved, and the tasks that can or cannot be delegated.

Won't I lose control?

Loss of control is a very common reason that people give for not delegating.

As we have said before, accountability cannot be delegated, so there must be some control to ensure a successful outcome. The difficulty is that delegation often involves some passing of authority to make independent decisions. Consider the following scene:

On Monday last, you delegated a job to one of your people, Janet. It is now Wednesday afternoon and you are sitting at your desk wondering how the job is going as it needs to be finished by Friday. You think, *I mustn't abdicate. I need to show some interest so I'll go and see how Janet is getting along.* So, off you go, good intentions and all, to Janet's desk. There she is, beavering away and you say something like, 'Hello, Janet. How's that job going that I gave you?'

Does this sound familiar?

Assume you are 'Janet'. What would you reply?

_____

_____

_____

_____

_____

_____

_____

There are three standard replies to this type of 'control':

- 'Fine'.
- 'Okay'.
- 'All right'.

Did you use any of them?

So, why *should* these be standard replies? The answer to this lies in what the delegatee is actually thinking. They do *not* usually see the manager as the helpful, caring individual he or she would like to think. They are thinking, *You gave me the job to do. Let me DO it. I know where your office is if I need you.*

AVOID OVER-CONTROL

Do you remember 'Long John Silver' in 'Treasure Island'? Most people visualise him with a parrot on his shoulder.

The manager can appear rather like *Long John Silver's parrot* – perching on their shoulder, squawking occasionally, without giving much useful input!

Whilst the manager may well get some information on progress through probing, ask yourself what effect the interruption had on the motivational state of the delegatee. How would *you* feel?

We are not saying that you should never ask someone how a dele-gated job is going. If the person is the sort who would never tell you no matter how difficult they were finding some aspect of the task, then a word when passing their desk might just prompt a question that would deal with the difficulty.

We know that abdication is relinquishing control entirely, and that's wrong. There is then the danger of over-control by us – Long John Silver's parrot! So how on earth do you let go without losing control?

HOW TO AVOID LOSING CONTROL

Involve the delegatee in the whole process of control! You are trusting them to do the job, and trusting them with the authority to make decisions. Trust them to help you develop an effective control system to ensure that the job will be completed successfully. The key task here is really to decide, ideally together, on *effective checkpoints* in order to:

- monitor (and, if need be, influence) progress to ensure that the var-ious stages, and the overall result that you need is achieved on time and to the right standards

29

- discuss/review any major decisions to ensure that the criteria have been adequately met
- reassure the person who is doing the task that things are progressing as they should.

> **LETTING GO WITHOUT LOSING CONTROL**
>
> **Delgating day-to-day control (with realistic limits) to the delegatee is *not* losing control.**

If you are wondering HOW to go about the process of actually setting up the control system for the task, look at Chapter 10 which is devoted to the topic of 'Control without interference'.

It's quicker to do it myself, isn't it?

The answer is, 'Probably, yes!'

As we have said before, time is always at a premium and deadlines are usually tight. So it is not too surprising that this is a common TRAP. It is most likely to occur when there is a job to be done that only you have done before. The thinking goes something like, *It will take me two hours to do this myself but it will take four hours for Harry to sort it out. There's not much time so I'll do it.*

THE 'ROUNDABOUT' PROBLEM

You can find yourself on a roundabout – it will *always* be quicker to do it yourself until you take the time to show someone else how to do it. Assuming that the job *can* be delegated, at some point you need to jump off the roundabout!

Very often, regular tasks fall into this category of 'roundabout' jobs. For example, management reports, budget/cost control, departmental meetings, etc.

Suppose you produce a management report every week that takes three hours to compile. The *first* time that you delegate it to, say, a team member, it may well take considerably more than three hours for you to explain it, give some guidance on its completion, let them do it, then go through the draft with the person. Let's be pessimistic and say that the lead time from start to finish might be six hours (two hours from you and four hours from them). Next time they might do it in three hours and you only need spend one hour. You have saved two hours which you can use on something more important.

SO WHY DON'T WE DO IT?

- we might enjoy doing that task
- we hadn't thought about these 'roundabout' jobs in that way before.

We enjoy doing the task

Fair enough, but ask yourself, 'Is this what I *should* be doing with my time?'. It is a natural thing to prefer doing enjoyable work but unfortunately life isn't like that. If you are in doubt about a particular task, try asking yourself how *your* boss would view the two hours that you have spent doing it. This should help you decide if you are prioritising on the basis of enjoyment or of importance.

If there are more important things that you should be doing, then its time to 'let go'. That doesn't mean that you will be delegating *every* enjoyable job. In fact, doing this may well free up more of your time for other enjoyable and important jobs that cannot be delegated.

We hadn't thought about these 'roundabout' jobs in that way before

If you have now decided that there are 'roundabout' jobs that could and should be delegated, it may help to make a note of them here and set yourself a deadline by which you will have done it:

'Roundabout' jobs	Action and deadline

But I can do it better, can't I?

That's what we *like* to think! In some cases, of course, it is true. You may have greater knowledge and a higher level of skill as a result of your experience on that particular task. This is rather like the 'roundabout' tasks we talked about in the previous section. You will *always* have greater knowledge and skill until you give someone in the team the opportunity to grow, i.e. develop their own knowledge and skill on that task. Given that you choose a person with the necessary ability and motivation, and set up the controls effectively with the delegatee, then there is no reason to suppose that they will not do a good job.

However, this response can cover a much more significant problem – our own ego! Some people are **really** concerned about a situation in which the delegatee actually does a better job than the manager. The simple answer is 'So what?'. The trick is firstly, to recognise it and then *use* it.

Bill, the Transport Manager of a medium-sized manufacturing firm, was faced with a decision as to what departmental information or tasks, if any, should be computerised. The Production Director had raised the question but made it clear that the decision was very much within Bill's own sphere of responsibility. Bill's problem however was that he had a mortal fear of computers ('*He's not alone!*', we hear you say) and, whilst accepting that he should be considering better ways of handling information, his main concern was that some vital piece of information might get lost forever in the bowels of the computer, and he wouldn't have a clue what to do. Besides he wasn't at all sure about these 'newfangled contraptions' anyway. On the other hand, Bill knew from people in other organisations how effective computers could be in handling route-planning and vehicle maintenance information.

It would have been relatively easy for Bill to make a very superficial investigation then conclude that computerisation would not be of benefit. Bill had the guts NOT to take that route!

Despite his fear and reservations, he wanted to give the idea a chance at least. One of his supervisors, Dave, just happened to be something of a computer whiz-bang (they were his hobby), always on about them and what they can do. Bill accepted that, as far as computers were concerned, he was a babe in arms so he asked Dave to handle the investigation, **and told him why**.

To cut a long story short, Dave suggested that a computer would help in various areas including transport cost control and identifying the most effective routes for the lorry deliveries, arranged for a loan computer on trial, showed Bill how it operated, and helped him use it, so that Bill could form his own view. Not surprisingly, the computer and software were bought quite quickly.

You might be thinking, *That's all very well if you have got someone like a Dave*, but often we have! It's all about handling our own ego. Bill scored because he accepted that Dave would do a better job than he, as the manager, would do, and had the courage to admit that and let Dave do it.

If you were the Production Director or Dave, the Supervisor, would Bill (the Transport Manager) go up or down in your estimation?

But I won't be needed any more, will I?

This thinking can go something like *If I train a team member to do this, then they won't need me any more. They would be able to get rid of me and put Fred or Freda in my job at £5000 per year less than me.*

We wouldn't pretend that this has *never* happened but we would suggest it is highly unlikely. If you learn to delegate effectively, we believe that you are far more likely to be promoted than fired.

That statement deserves some justification – so why are you more likely to be promoted?

How senior managers view delegation

If we split the 'managerial' job at different levels into 'Technical Content' and 'Management Content', the proportional content would approximate to the graph shown in Figure 4.1.

So, for example, at the left-hand end, let's say we have a senior programmer who spends maybe 90 per cent of the time writing the advanced computer programs and the remaining 10 per cent on managerial activities such as deciding who will write which program, issuing the work, monitoring progress, query handling, etc.

In the middle of the organisation, managers may divide their time 50/50 as the managerial activities are more wide-ranging, and now take even more of the time.

33

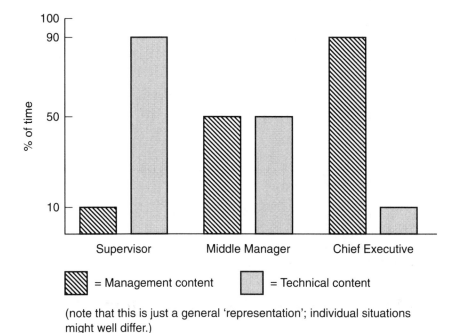

(note that this is just a general 'representation'; individual situations might well differ.)

Fig 4.1 How the role changes

At the top, we have a chief executive or whatever, who may be a technical 'expert' in one area of the business but typically has six directors reporting. Suppose the chief executive has come up through the sales ranks, they may well be an 'expert' in that area but they also have Production, Personnel, Finance, Marketing, and Administration reporting in to them. To do their job they *have* to delegate. In order to get there in the first place they have had to learn how to delegate. They didn't find it any easier than the rest of us. Try asking one!

A managing director known to both of us started a small plastics firm, having received his grounding as an apprentice then as a tool-maker. As the firm grew from the original twelve people, one of the hardest things he had to cope with was learning to 'let go'. He tried to be managing director and tool-maker all rolled into one and it simply did not work. He never forgot his background but, as time progressed, he understood that he knew less and less about his old role especially as technology progressed and newer machines were installed. Also, he was paying other people to do what he used to do, and he had to accept that he was no longer the tool-maker!

34

We would suggest that most senior managers have to go through this loop on their way up, and (hopefully) learn to cope with it. Consequently, most seem to understand the difficulties, but recognise and value the ability to delegate.

Put yourself in the position of senior manager or director. An opportunity for promotion occurs. Who would you promote – the expert or the delegator?

So, in conclusion, if you learn to delegate, and develop your team in the process, when a promotion opportunity for you arises, there is someone capable of stepping into your role, minimising the disruption.

SUMMARY – CHAPTER 4

- Most managers do not delegate enough
- Developing a positive attitude towards delegation is vital
- Avoid abdication or over-control, by allowing the delegatee to control (within agreed limits)
- Consider whether any 'roundabout' jobs should/could be delegated
- Handle your own ego – accept that someone in the team may do a better job on a particular task than you
- As your career progresses, your own technical expertise often becomes less important than your ability to manage

5

The real barrier to letting go

Overview of this chapter

In this chapter, we will look at the *overriding* reason for not delegating enough, and decide what can be done to deal with it.

What are the objectives for this chapter?

When you have read this chapter, you should:

- understand the overriding reason for not delegating
- know how to minimise or handle it.

What is covered in this chapter?

- The major barrier that stops us delegating.
- The power of **FEAR** and the effect it has on us.
- How to minimise or handle it.
- Being realistic about it.

The major barrier that stops us delegating

The reasons for not delegating which were given in the last chapter came from managers who said either that they did not delegate at all, or did not delegate enough. We then looked at each of these and tried to decide when it might be a valid reason for not delegating, or when it became an excuse!

For example, a new manager might quite rightly feel that he or she cannot delegate important tasks initially because their knowledge of the team is minimal at that point (a reason). However, after six months, it is no longer a reason; it has become an excuse for not delegating. So why do these valid reasons sometimes turn into excuses.

!!! FEAR !!!

We really do have to question our own motives for failing to delegate and truthfully classify the causes as:

■ genuine reasons
■ excuses born usually out of fear.

36 Look back at the activity at the beginning of Chapter 4, 'Most managers do not delegate enough'. If you identified any of the factors there as excuses, do you think that 'fear' is at the bottom of it?

The power of fear and the effect it has on us

Fear is an extremely powerful emotion. Real fear can produce all sorts of reactions in us. Think about a situation that can easily produce fear in anyone being told that you are to give a talk to agroup of people.

Most people are nervous about standing up in front of a group and giving a talk; some more so than others. Fairly common reactions when we first stand up include sweaty palms, dry throat, shaky hands or legs, fear of 'drying-up', etc. and we think, *Why me! Other people seem to be able to do this without any problem.* NOT TRUE! They just don't *appear* to be nervous.

Some years ago, I knew someone who was well known in public life and spent a great deal of his time talking to large audiences. On one occasion I was with him before he 'went on'. He managed to go through around five cigarettes in as many minutes and was shaking like a leaf. I knew him well enough to be able to say, '*You have been doing this for years and you know how they react to you. Why on earth are you so nervous?*'

Back came the reply which I have never forgotten. '*I'm always like this. Every audience is an unknown quantity so I don't know how they will react.*

The day that I am not nervous will be the one on which I will do a lousy job, because I will have stopped caring how they view me.' He then 'went on' and, as though some sort of switch had been thrown, gave his usual polished, high-quality 'performance'.

The same is true for delegation. The day we are not somewhat nervous about delegating is the day we have stopped caring how others view us. So really what we are saying is that it is okay to be nervous but not to a point where it stops you delegating the responsibility and authority.

THE 'INDISPENSABILITY' TRAP

We all know that nobody is totally indispensable but we like to believe that we are. We want to feel needed and there is nothing wrong with that. However it can go too far as illustrated in the following situation.

The scene is the administration office of a small engineering company. It was before the days of computers and the invoices were typed out, and sent out by one lady, who also recorded the payments when they came in. When she went off for a couple of days' holiday she took the invoice books with her! Nobody else knew her system and she certainly wasn't going to let anyone 'interfere' with it. You may well be thinking, *What on earth was her manager doing to let her get away with that?* However, she had tried to make herself indispensable.

Indispensability can be by design, as in the case above, born out of some sort of fear, or it can occur by accident.

Suppose you have just completed a project. A new one comes into the department and your boss asks you to handle it as you are now free. Within a month you can become the company expert on the project because only you have been involved. This can produce a very comfortable feeling. *They can't get rid of me because nobody knows anything about this but me.* However, there is another side to that coin – you may be virtually indispensable but how do you think the senior manager might view your situation?

Note your thoughts down here:

_____

_____

_____

_____

37

> **THE DANGER OF INDISPENSABILITY**
>
> **If you become indispensable, either by design or by accident . . . you may also make yourself unpromotable!**

How to minimise or handle it

'Minimising' really involves understanding the causes of the natural fear that accompanies delegation. 'Handling' means doing something about it.

From your earlier work you will have classified your reasons for not delegating as 'an excuse' or 'a valid reason'.

EXCUSES

You have already gone a long way towards dealing with these by being honest enough to admit it (if only to yourself). If you really consider the benefits of delegating, they invariably outweigh the disadvantages. So we are talking 'attitude' here. If you decide that you *want* to delegate, then you will.

List your views of the benefits of delegating versus snags and see how it looks.

Benefits	Snags
_____	_____
_____	_____
_____	_____
_____	_____
_____	_____

REASONS

Valid reasons for not delegating might be applicable at this point in time. However they can often be handled if you choose to do so. Many of the common reasons for not delegating were covered in Chapter 4, together with possible actions to help.

Now look at the items that you classed as 'valid reasons'. If any were similar to those in Chapter 4 then consider whether the actions suggested would help you.

List your thoughts below, and, if possible, include a deadline for action.

Example

Reason: Mary lacks experience of the task (but could do it).

Action and deadline: Allow plenty of time (to explain and do it), provide support, in mid March when quiet.

Valid reason   **Action and deadline**

39

Being realistic about fear

Some element of fear when delegating is natural for *both* parties. As manager, you are accountable and do not want the task to go wrong. The delegatee does not want to let you down either. Fear of a failure cannot really be eliminated until the task has been successfully completed. By setting up an effective control system, the chances of failure are minimised AND SO IS THE FEAR!

SUMMARY – CHAPTER 5

- The major barrier to delegating is . . . FEAR!!!

- Separate 'valid reasons' from 'excuses'

- Beware of the 'Indispensibility Trap'

- Decide actions and deadlines to handle valid reasons for not delegating

Choosing the right task to delegate

Overview of this chapter

A common concern for managers hinges on actually choosing which jobs to delegate. In this chapter, we will look at the tasks that can and can't be delegated.

What are the objectives for this chapter?

When you have read this chapter, you should:

- know how to set effective objectives
- know how to choose appropriate tasks for delegation
- have identified tasks suitable for delegation, if you have the opportunity to delegate.

What is covered in this chapter?

- What can or cannot be delegated.
- Deciding your objective.
- Deciding which tasks to delegate.

What can or cannot be delegated?

This question is a tough one for most managers. Very few people find it easy to make this choice. There are few hard and fast rules because so much depends on the abilities and experience of the people involved, and the complexity of the possible tasks.

This chapter will concentrate on possible TASKS; the following chapter looks at choosing the right PERSON.

WHAT CANNOT BE DELEGATED?

Let's deal with that one first. If you remember from Chapter 3, the **one thing that you cannot delegate is 'ACCOUNTABILITY'**. It has to be said that some managers do try! Do you recall the story of the Sales Manager who tried to delegate accountability?

As the manager of the unit, you are accountable for all of the work carried out by your people whether it is 'assigned' or 'delegated' .

WHAT CAN BE DELEGATED?

You can't delegate accountability, but you can delegate

- a task that is part of your job
- the responsibility for successful completion
- the authority to make independent decisions.

'That's all very well, but that means I can delegate everything, doesn't it?' you might say. Would you really want to delegate the overall control of the work of the department for which you are accountable? Probably not. This would be seen as abdication, not delegation.

'Surely some tasks are more appropriate for delegation than others, aren't they?' may be your next question. Yes. Going back to the benefits of delegating, several factors were identified (making better use of your time, developing your team, motivation, 'better' decisions by using any expert knowledge in your team). These areas will help us to identify possible tasks for delegation which will hopefully produce the result that we want. Selection of the actual task to delegate depends very much on YOUR OBJECTIVE, i.e. the result that you want the delegated activity to achieve. So the first thing to look at is how to set an objective.

Deciding which tasks to delegate will be covered in a later section of this chapter.

Setting the objective

Setting effective objectives is a key skill in any sphere, not just in delegation. In this section we will look at how to do this.

To enable you to compare your approach with ours, please write an objective for something that you need to do at work over the next week. (Any task will do; it does not have to relate to delegation. The content isn't important.)

43

FINDING THE RIGHT LEVEL FOR THE OBJECTIVE

If the objective that we set is aimed at the wrong level, then there is a strong danger of falling into 'fire fighting', and ignoring 'fire prevention'. Fire fighting is often caused by time pressures on the manager. A crisis occurs, it needs quick action and that is often where it stops. We have dealt with the EFFECT, but not with the CAUSE.

Many people have a general idea of what they want to achieve when delegating, e.g. *I must have this report done by tonight so I'll ask Frank to handle the figure work for me.* Whilst this is a fairly common situation, is it right? Frank might help to solve the current time problem for the manager but really this is 'fire fighting' . The next time this situation occurs, poor old Frank will be at it again.

The manager might be on a roundabout; jumping from one crisis to another, without ever really solving the REAL problem.

Whilst this report must be done, at some point the manager needs to jump off the roundabout. The real problem for the manager here may be, *I don't have enough time to do what I need to do.* The objective has switched from simply getting the report done, to a much wider issue with many more options.

Consequently, the manager really has two objectives; getting the report completed by tonight (the effect) and finding ways of making more time available for what the manager really needs to do (the cause). The first is urgent but is 'fire fighting' , the second is 'fire prevention' and far more significant.

 Look back at the objective you listed on the previous page. Are you 'on the roundabout'? (responding to some sort of crisis by 'fire fighting' ?) If this is the case, write an objective that will help you to 'prevent the fire' in the future.

_____

_____

_____

RESULTS VERSUS ACTIVITIES

One of the most common pitfalls that occurs when trying to produce worthwhile objectives is that of confusing ACTIVITIES with RESULTS.

Suppose a manager wants to buy an extra personal computer for the department. The objective would often look something like:

44

> *Prepare a report, by the end of this month, for the Finance Director on departmental computer resources.*

So what can easily happen is that the report contains a detailed analysis of existing resources and requirements with the benefits to the manager/department clearly shown. This is fairly typical for an objective, but preparing a report is an activity, not a result!

Ask yourself what RESULT the manager wants. Probably to persuade the Finance Director to *approve* the purchase of an extra computer.

45

What effect do you think that result-orientation might have on the situation?

_____

_____

_____

_____

_____

_____

_____

_____

_____

The manager might think a presentation stands more chance than a posted report, but keep the report there as hard copy for the Director. This is now clearly a 'selling' situation so the report might major on benefits to the Finance Director, rather than to just the department/manager.

> **OBJECTIVES SHOULD SHOW:**
>
> **the RESULT required**
> **(i.e. convince the Finance Director)**
>
> **rather than**
>
> **the ACTIVITY**
> **(i.e. prepare a report on computers)**

HOW DO YOU WRITE AN EFFECTIVE OBJECTIVE?

As we have already said, it must be result-oriented. There are also some other guidelines that help but sadly, they are often not used.

An effective objective should be **CLEAR, MEASURABLE** (if possible), and **REALISTIC**.

Clear

If you write an objective for yourself, you *know* what you mean. Clarity becomes very important when producing an objective for someone else.

Suppose that you are about to purchase a new house. Let's say that you and your partner want a house 'with some character'. Both of you have probably discussed this and know what it means (at least that's the plan!) If, however, you give your requirements to an estate agent, he or she may well have an entirely different view of 'character'. So you and your partner wanted a house with Tudor beams and leaded windows; the estate agent sends you details of a condemned wreck with 'bags of potential'. Isn't that always the way? The problem is that the requirements were not made clear to the person who has to do the job.

When delegating, it is vital that you produce an unambiguous objective for the delegatee. It might mean being a bit more specific than if you were writing it for yourself but it's worth it to achieve the right result. You may be thinking that this section is blindingly obvious. Perhaps, but there are many instances of delegation problems arising from lack of clarity.

The old fork-lift truck at an engineering firm had seen better days, to put it mildly. The motor gave a good impression of a pneumatic drill! The foreman had been complaining about the state of the truck for some time; it was not dangerous but simply 'past it', and spending a lot of time under repair.

The production manager asked the foreman (who reported to him) to *'look into the purchase of a new fork-lift truck for the machine shop as soon as possible'*. Breathing a huge sigh of relief, off went the foreman, highly motivated (at that point), spoke to three sales representatives, arranged some very rapid demonstrations of fork-lift trucks, and gave the details of the best truck to the purchasing manager, asking him to order it right away as the production manager said it was needed *'as soon as possible'*. This the purchasing manager duly did.

Thinking no more about it, the purchasing manager sent a copy of the order through to the production manager and duly debited his production department capital equipment budget (which was the way that their system worked). On receipt of the copy order, the production manager reacted ever so slightly (roughly equivalent to level 9 on the Richter scale). The poor old foreman was summoned to his office, with accompanying threats of doom and destruction, and the production manager demanded to know *'why the foreman had gone 'over his head'?'*

Totally thrown, the foreman said, *'You asked me to get a new one as soon as possible and I thought this would do it quickly'*.

Back came the reply from the production manager, *'I wanted you to LOOK INTO IT as soon as possible and make a recommendation to me. Not just go out and BUY the damn thing! The purchasing manager said that you told her that I wanted it straight away'*.

'That's what you said when you gave me the job', said the foreman.

47

Whatever the rights and wrongs, the objective was simply not clear to the foreman who was given the job. Whilst both parties share the responsibility for this misunderstanding, the manager bears the lion's share. Largely because people do not want to appear silly by asking if they have got the right message. He should have ensured that the objective was clear, i.e. 'The fork-lift truck needs to be replaced. Make a recommendation to me by the end of the week as to which one you think that we should buy. I will discuss it with you and then place an order'. In fairness, being wise after the event is always easy. Everyone who reads this book can probably think of parallels where the objective simply was not clear to the person who had to do the job.

Measurable (if possible)

This is probably one of the most difficult aspects of objective setting. Some objectives are relatively easy to make measurable, e.g. a sales objective might be 'to sell 50 hum-grummets by the end of next month'. However life is not usually so simple.

Suppose that you decide to ask a member of your team to run the routine monthly departmental meeting next month in your absence. To say something like, 'Run an effective departmental meeting on my behalf next month', is probably not enough if the person has never done it before. For instance, what does 'effective' mean?

For the objective to be measurable by the person who is going to do the job, you would need to explain how to measure 'effective'. If the objective lacks measurability, try asking yourself, 'What *result* do I want from this?' It may be that the people at the meeting will have to prepare an action plan so you expect the attendees to agree specific actions with deadlines for completion within one month, and with a specific person responsible for each action. Now the objective has become rather more measurable than it was before.

Realistic

Again, it may on the surface seem obvious to say that an objective must be realistic, i.e. achievable. There can be a major trap here. When estimating times, we often use ourselves as the benchmark, i.e. how long would it take me to do this? What is realistic for you as the manager might not be so for the person to whom you are delegating. You might be able to prepare a presentation in two hours but, if they have only limited experience, they will certainly need significantly more time than two hours. Always ask yourself, 'What is realistic for *them?*'

So far we have only mentioned time in this context. Realistic expectations about the results are also important. You might find presentations relatively easy to deliver because you have been doing it for years. If they have only made one or two, they are still going to be nervous about it, especially if it is on your behalf.

AN EFFECTIVE OBJECTIVE SHOULD BE:

- **Clear to the person who has to do the job.**
- **Measurable so that the person will know when it has been successfully achieved.**
- **Realistic i.e. achievable, for the person who will do the job, in terms of both**
  – the results you expect, and
  – the time you have allowed.

An effective objective should show the **deadline**, and **any constraints**, in addition to being result-oriented.

The deadline

It is important to include the deadline in any objective for a delegated task as it prompts the person to plan time accordingly to ensure that the job is completed on time. If you do not set any sort of deadline, then you cannot complain if the job seems to take forever.

Try to avoid 'as soon as possible'. People really don't know whether that means an hour, day, week, or month. Try to make a sensible estimate of the time you believe that the job will take, add some extra time if the person has not done the job before, and then discuss the suggested deadline with them. This is to ensure that *they* believe it to be a realistic time scale. If they have no knowledge of the task then they will rely heavily on your judgement of the time required, so try to be fair.

Any constraints

49

Constraints usually exist in most situations, especially in delegated tasks. When you delegate authority, it is usually within certain limits but strangely, these limits (constraints) are sometimes just not made clear to the person.

'Ben, we need to buy 20 new printers for our PC's. Would you contact our usual supplier and negotiate a discount for me, and place the order'.

A couple of hours later . . . 'Good news, Karen. I have agreed a 6 per cent discount and the printers will be here in two weeks'.

'Oh no, Ben. I expected you to get at least 15 per cent on an order of that size . . .'

All that Karen needed to do was TELL Ben that before he contacted the supplier. So why don't some managers tell people what the limits might be. Sometimes they are not sure themselves. Sometimes managers assume that the person knows what they are or can work them out. Sometimes they do not think about limits until it is too late.

There is another rather more manipulative reason. The thinking goes something like *'If I don't set a limit, they might do better than I expect'*. The reality is often the reverse (as it was with the discount above). People will set their own limits unless you tell them otherwise, and they may be different to yours.

> **AN EFFECTIVE OBJECTIVE SHOULD:**
> - be result-oriented (rather than activity-oriented)
> - show the deadline for completion
> - and any constraints or limits on authority.

What follows is an example of an objective that meets all of the criteria we have covered.

> *Order, from XYZ Limited, 20 new laser printers to suit our personal computers for delivery within four weeks, having negotiated a discount of at least 15% on normal one-off price to us.*

This might appear somewhat stark but how often have you seen woolly objectives cause difficulties for people. Decide whether you think it is result-oriented, clear, realistic (we can only assume so as it is an example), measurable, showing the deadline and any constraints. We think that it is rather better than the 'objective' that Karen gave to Ben in the earlier example.

Due to the fact that objectives are so important, a self-assessment activity follows which will help you to practise setting objectives based on the ideas we have covered so far. This is optional, of course, but is strongly recommended.

 A situation is outlined opposite. Assume that you are the Senior Customer Liaison Officer. Read through the situation then list what you see to be your objectives for the next three months.

50

THE SITUATION

The company

Manufactures personal computers and sells them direct to customers, ready loaded with the software required by the users, and tested. The company has been in existence since 1983 and has established a name for service and quality.

The situation

You work in the Sales Department as the Senior Customer Liaison Officer, dealing with 20 major accounts. There are two other Customer Liaison staff who deal with the remaining accounts in the UK, splitting the area as 'North' and 'South'. You joined the company two months ago from another firm where you were in Customer Liaison, so this job represented a promotion for you. You are good at your job and have established yourself quickly with the major customers, where your contacts see you as very helpful. Generally, you get on well with people, but often 'clash' with the Production Control Manager over customer complaint issues (rather than as a result of any personality clash). When you 'chase' him over customer complaints due to late delivery, he takes it personally and sees you as a 'company policeman' rather than as a colleague. At the end of the day, you get what action you need usually.

51

Your job description

Overall purpose. To arrange for any concerns that major account customers may have to be resolved promptly and efficiently, i.e. 'promote customer satisfaction'.

(a) Clarify and route major account customer queries to the appropriate person for action, and monitor progress until resolved.

(b) Clarify and route major account customer complaints to the appropriate manager for action, and ensure that they are handled promptly and efficiently. The support of the appropriate Divisional Director can be requested by the job holder if necessary.

(c) Arrange meetings if appropriate with major account customers to deal with queries and/or complaints. This includes date/time, venue, attendees, and agenda, together with prior briefing of the company attendees.

(d) Produce monthly reports of major account customer queries and complaints, with copies to all directors and managers.

(e) Ensure that all files/documents are correctly filed (computer or filing cabinet) and immediately accessible to directors and managers.

The issues. After your two months settling-in period (which has gone well), the Sales Manager, to whom you report, has asked you to suggest your objectives for the next three months. You have given the situation some thought and have identified a number of areas for consideration, (in addition to just 'doing your job').

(a) You feel that, whilst complaints are generally handled well, the customer should receive a telephone response within twenty-four hours, followed up by a confirmation letter from you. The Sales Manager and directors would support this improvement.

(b) Whilst your contacts at the major accounts seem fairly happy, you believe that there should be some form of proper customer satisfaction check after complaints have been handled. At the moment, the complaint just disappears.

(c) The current monthly reports could be improved. You think that 'monthly' is too long and that they should also show action to *prevent* re-occurrence of the complaint. The Sales Admin. typist is fully occupied at the moment so could not handle extra typing.

Your suggested objectives for the Senior Customer Liaison Officer

_____

_____

_____

_____

_____

_____

_____

_____

_____

_____

_____

Our view of possible objectives for the Senior Customer Liaison Officer

1 The issues that need to be addressed

(a) Improve the speed of response to customer complaints, and follow with a confirmation letter.

(b) Devise some form of customer satisfaction check with major account customers once complaints have been handled.

(c) Modify the reporting procedure without adversely affecting the current high work load of the Sales Admin. typist. (Workload is high 'at the moment'.)

(d) Improve the working relationship with the Production Manager, with help if necessary but without resorting to 'big stick' tactics. (This issue is often missed. People seem aware of it but don't actually DO anything about it.)

2 The objectives for the Senior Customer Liaison Officer

[Criteria = result-oriented, clear, measurable (if possible), and realistic].

(a) Improve the handling of customer complaints by responding by telephone within twenty-four hours of receiving the complaint, followed up by a confirmation letter from Customer Liaison. Timing: confirm management approval within two weeks and implement once approval is confirmed, by end of first month.

(b) Develop, gain approval by management for, and implement some form of Customer Satisfaction check (questionnaire, or telephone conversation, etc.) for use by Customer Liaison with major account customers, to ensure that they are happy with the service received, by end of second month. Build results into the reporting procedure by end of third month (see also objective c).

(c) Alter the format of the existing Customer Liaison Monthly Report to show actions taken in each case, to prevent re-occurrence of complaints, and amend frequency to 'fortnightly'. Timing: agree with Sales Manager/typist for implementation to commence at the beginning of the third month, to avoid causing a typing overload 'at the moment'.

(d) Improve the working relationship (so no longer viewed as 'company policeman') with the Production Manager by a personal discussion to help him to understand the need for prompt delivery of items on time, reducing complaints and consequent pressure from Customer Liaison, (ideally without bringing the 'management guns' into play), by end of first month.

How did your objectives compare with our version?

Ignoring the actual wording, which is likely to differ, were your objectives result-oriented, clear, measurable (if possible), and realistic?

Are there any improvements that you can make with regard to the way that you write objectives? If so, list them below, for future reference.

_____

_____

_____

_____

_____

_____

_____

54

_____

If you identified any possible improvements, please look back at the work-related objective that you wrote at the beginning of this section 'Setting the objective' and rewrite it accordingly.

_____

_____

_____

_____

_____

_____

_____

As you know, it takes time to produce an effective objective but we believe that the small amount of extra time is well worth the outcome. We hope that, having worked through this section, you agree.

Deciding which tasks to delegate

You know that responsibility and authority can be delegated. However, this does not help much when trying to decide *which tasks* to delegate. As the decision rests on so many situational factors, we cannot say you should delegate this or that. What we *can* do is to identify some 'triggers' which might prompt some ideas as to which tasks you might consider as possible contenders for delegation.

These 'triggers' as to possible contenders for delegation link to the benefits of delegating and fall into four categories. Tasks that, if delegated, would:

- help you to make better use of your time
- enable you to develop members of your team
- help you to motivate people in the team
- enable 'better' decisions, by allowing you more time for major decisions or by using the greater skills/knowledge of your people.

55

TASKS THAT WOULD HELP YOU TO MAKE BETTER USE OF YOUR TIME

What am I here for?

Before we get on to the possible tasks, let's look at the phrase 'better use of your time'. Time is a precious commodity, and nobody seems to ever have enough of it. There are only twenty-four hours in a day and whatever we do, nothing can change that. What we *can* do is to ensure as far as possible that the time we do have is spent wisely.

Have you ever arrived home after a very hectic day at work and thought to yourself, *I am tired out! I spent the whole day rushing from one thing to another but I don't really feel that I achieved much?* It is not an uncommon reaction, once in a while at least. Occasionally, we all probably feel like that. However some people seem to make a career out of it. They permanently rush blindly around, rather like a chicken with no head, producing lots of frenetic 'activity' but not too many 'results', i.e. the things they are paid as a manager to produce.

So, in order to look at making better use of our time, the first question must be 'how should I be spending my time?'

A delegate of ours on a training course once said that she believed every manager should have a large sign on their desk that reads:

> ## WHAT AM I HERE FOR?

We think that she is right. All of us lose sight of that occasionally and some people don't even appear to have asked themselves the question – ever!

Have you ever encountered the type of manager who, when asked to make a decision under crisis conditions, staunchly refuses? Forms requiring authorisation appear to go into a 'black hole' (the manager's office), and are never seen again. Yet this same manager will spend two hours playing with the wording of an internal memo of yours that really isn't important. Paid to make decisions, but prefers to spend the time on relatively unimportant activities!

How do you spend your time now?

Jot down the main things **that you actually do** in the course of a week or month, whichever you prefer.

_____

_____

_____

_____

_____

_____

_____

_____

_____

_____

_____

Assuming that you have the opportunity to delegate, now answer, in the space below, the question 'What am I here for?' (Just key words or phrases are sufficient.)

_____

_____

_____

_____

Now compare the last two activities and mark those in the first, 'How do you spend your time now?', which directly contribute to 'What am I here for?'. The 80/20 rule often applies to this comparison. Twenty per cent of the things we actually do produce 80 per cent of the results for which we are paid. This doesn't mean that the other 80 per cent of tasks that occupy our time are unimportant. They may be necessary but are *less* important than the key 20 per cent.

If your objective in delegating is to make better use of your time, then look at the 80 per cent of less important tasks. There may well be contenders in this list that, if delegated, would allow you more time to spend on the top 20 per cent.

But what about the urgent jobs? They still have to be done, and it may be quicker to do it myself

Agreed. But the real question is, 'How much time are they worth?'. This is not a book on time management as such, but we are talking about making better use of your time via delegation. Sometimes managers seem to prioritise on the basis of 'urgency' rather than 'importance'. Consequently it is easy to fall into the trap of spending a lot of time on an urgent task that is simply not important.

57

You might just be thinking to yourself *Oh, come on. Time is too precious for people to fall into an obvious trap like that.* Let us give you an example.

This particular organisation was moving to new offices in one week. A meeting was held and there were two items on the agenda.

- A new computer system covering invoicing and credit control that concerned everyone in the meeting. They would input to it and/or receive output from it.
- Management car parking at the new office site. The nine managers concerned were at the meeting.

One agenda item took one and a half hours, the other took ten minutes. Which was which? Yes, you are probably right!

After the meeting, the chair was asked why management car parking took one and a half hours, whereas the computer system was only given ten minutes.

'Well, it's urgent. We are moving next week and the computer system doesn't come in until the end of that week.'

'Okay, agreed, it's urgent. How important is it then?'

'Very important; it's dealing with people and they get very concerned about things like this.'

'Nine managers need spaces. How many spaces are there in the new management car park please?'
'Well, um, er, twelve actually.'

Now why do you think it took one and a half hours when there were nine people and twelve spaces? The chair had given people the 'green light' to discuss it so the discussion hinged on how near or far someone was from the main door! 'I have been here longest so I should be nearest the door, etc. etc'.

The issue was urgent but not important; everyone would have a space, and the layout was such that the furthest person would have been forty feet from the door at most. (Considerably nearer than the rest of the staff who would be in a car park some 300 yards down the road.)

How much time would YOU have allowed for that agenda item knowing what you now know? Ten minutes, if that?

The chair really hadn't thought much about the importance of it so was far too short of time to have an adequate discussion on the computer system that was both urgent *and* important.

The moral is that IMPORTANT tasks probably fall into your top 20 per cent – the tasks that produce the results. The URGENT tasks may or may not fall into this category. If the task is urgent but unimportant, do you have to spend time doing it? 'Urgent' does not necessarily mean 'immediate'. Once you have taken the time to delegate it properly to someone, they can then handle it, or a similar task if and when it arises again. It may be slower the first time but, after that, you are gaining time for more important things.

58

Routine, time-consuming tasks

Most of us have a host of routine tasks that just tend to get taken for granted. For instance, preparing the agenda for a monthly departmental meeting, or producing a weekly report. We are used to doing them and to fitting them in with our other work, but nevertheless they can take a considerable proportion of our time to complete. This time could well be used more effectively on the more important tasks.

Very often, we don't even think about delegating these tasks and it is worth considering doing so. You may find them **routine** because you have been doing them regularly and for so long. A member of your team may find the task quite interesting, or even challenging.

'Tweaking' tasks that your staff have done

Be honest. Do you spend any time making minor alterations to work your staff have produced? Some managers seem to spend a significant amount of time doing just this. If this is the case, you need to think carefully about WHY this is happening. If problems occur with work that is part of their normal role, is there a training need? It may be that a small amount of time spent on explaining the requirements in detail may save considerable checking/modification by you. If, however, the difficulties result from a delegated task, then perhaps the briefing was at fault; perhaps less clear than it might have been. Whilst we do not want to treat people as though they are idiots, it is all too easy to go too far the other way. Assuming that they know enough about the delegated task, or will be able to work it out, is a common failing.

One last thought – there is another possible reason for this. Some people change things that their staff do *on principle*, i.e. because they like to wield a bit of power, and be seen to be doing so. Often there is no need to make changes but it makes them feel good by doing so. If you decide that you might be guilty of this, you are already a long way towards solving it; you have admitted it to yourself. Now do something about it. Try delegating a bit of that power, i.e. some responsibility and/or authority, and see what effect it has on the motivation of your staff. Hopefully, you will be pleasantly surprised.

59

Tasks that you enjoy doing

This is a hard one, especially as you have a certain amount of power that can enable you to hang on to these particular jobs. To relinquish tasks that you enjoy doing is called 'becoming a manager!' Earth-shattering, eh!

You might enjoy it, and there's nothing wrong with enjoying something. However, is it something that you *should* be doing, enjoyable or not? If, again, you feel that really you should not be doing it, then it's just got to go. It might help to think about it in terms of making you more time to do the more important things. Probably some of these are equally enjoyable. So you are very unlikely to delegate all of the tasks that you enjoy doing anyway.

Tasks that are really part of a team member's role

Do you remember the story at the start of this book; the one about David's promotion? He was taught a fairly hard lesson when he got involved in (interfered with) something that was now part of Karen's role. Paul (the Managing Director) taught him that he was not where he should be, or doing what he should be doing.

Few people start off as 'managers'. A fairly typical career path might go something like Personnel Officer, Senior Personnel Officer,

Personnel Manager (not necessarily in the same organisation, of course). Consequently, the person whose career has progressed in this way has a reasonable knowledge of the work carried out by the team members they now manage. They might also be very good at doing some of those tasks but that is not what they are now paid for. They are paid to *manage* the department, not to DO the work that should be done by the team.

This is often a hard task for a newly promoted manager. A new manager is very familiar with the work in the old role from which he or she has now moved; much less familiar with the new management role. There is a very real danger that, out of interest, skill, or sheer fear of the unknown, the new manager spends far too much time helping with or doing the work that should be done by team members.

If you are particularly good at a particular task or tasks for which the team are now responsible, consider coaching the people concerned to help them to increase their own skills and knowledge. You may well find this enjoyable and it will help their own motivation, assuming that they want to increase their ability in this task. In this way, the task will be carried out effectively and to the standards that you require. You should then be able to let them get on with it. Try to remember that the task is part of *their* job, not yours.

Tasks that cause problems in your absence

These really fall into two categories; those you know about, and those which you do not.

Let's look first at those you know about. When you return to the office, someone comes over to you and explains that they had (or are having) difficulties with whatever task. The first question needs to be WHY are they having difficulties with it. There can be many reasons but here are the most common:

■ they do not know what to do next.
(This is really about your original explanation, or their understanding of it. Improving their level of understanding should do the trick.)
■ they lack the confidence to proceed, without approval from you.

Few people want to let down their manager. Even though you may have given them the authority to make the decisions necessary for progress, they still have that nagging feeling that they should check. Decide whether they are justified or not. If a major stumbling block has arisen that you did not anticipate, accept the situation. No one can anticipate everything – you are human too. Give them some guidelines to help them both now and when they have to do this task again in the future.

If you feel that the delay (due to their need to check with you) was not really justified, try to find out why they are feeling as they are. Basically, they probably just lack the confidence to proceed alone. Something is obviously bothering them even though you believed that they were capable of doing whatever was necessary to proceed. Occasionally, when someone is being briefed to do a task in your absence, they will agree to do it, just to 'keep the boss happy'. A team member might *agree* to try and do it but that does not mean that they necessarily *feel comfortable* about making the necessary decisions. You obviously had faith in the person (otherwise you wouldn't have given them the job to do in the first place) but did you make this plain when you briefed them? If you sounded unsure, they probably felt unsure as a result.

It is also worth thinking about any previous similar situations involving this person or this task, which might have produced this lack of confidence.

The scene is a school hall, many years ago. Mark, aged 12, was doing gymnastics in a physical education lesson. He had to jump a low bench, somersault over a gymnastic box, and finally vault over a pommel horse. He jumped the bench cleanly, managed a superb somersault over the box, but mistimed the beat board and crashed into the vaulting horse, ending up sitting on the floor in front of it. The teacher, who was extremely strict, called the lad six different sorts of clumsy idiot for mistiming the vault, without any mention of what he had done well up to that point, and basically made him look silly in front of the rest of his class. Mark was sent back for another try at it.

What happened this time? Well, the lad promptly tripped over the first bench and fell flat on his face because, in my opinion, the teacher has smashed his confidence to bits, and you need a bit of confidence in order to do it. The teacher was 'not happy'.

Like the rest of us, no teacher is perfect; if the account is accurate, perhaps he was just having an off-day, but it had a dramatic effect.

Four years later, Mark loved sports, but hated gymnastics and anything to do with it. (That particular teacher was not exactly 'top of the pops' for Mark either!) Not too surprising really.

Going back to delegation, ask yourself whether the person's lack of confidence could be due to an earlier failure that was perhaps not handled quite as well as it might have been.

Now for those tasks that cause difficulty in your absence, but about which you may never hear (unless you ask). There are two main reasons. The difficulty was eventually overcome so there is no *need* to tell you, or the difficulty is still there but the person does not *want* to tell you.

Without adequate controls, you may never know. To avoid this, it is vital to discuss *all* of the delegated jobs when you return.

The first reason mentioned previously is not really a problem. The person who had the job to do encountered difficulties, but found their own solution, i.e. used their initiative. The only issue might be that the job took rather longer than anticipated. Your discussion should uncover what actually happened.

The second reason is far more significant. No one enjoys admitting difficulties or even defeat. 'Oh, by the way, Janet, I thought that you might just like to know that I totally wrecked that presentation to the Managing Director whilst you were away. It's probably set your career back ten years. Is that okay?'

Some people go the other way and adopt the ostrich approach. When danger looms, bury your head in the sand and hope it goes away.

This often results in the philosophy that goes, 'If you don't ask, then I'm not going to tell you. With luck, it might just go away'.

As with the confidence issue in the earlier section, it is important to find out WHY the person feels this way. Do they simply not want to admit to having difficulties, or has something happened previously that deters them from doing so? Either way, an empathetic discussion should uncover the true situation, and enable you to then do something about it, both now and for any future jobs of a similar nature.

TASKS THAT HELP YOU TO DEVELOP MEMBERS OF YOUR TEAM

Not too many years ago, most managers seemed to think that 'development' was the responsibility of the Training Department; at least, that used to be the approach taken. If someone needed to learn something, then send them on a course.

More recently, the majority of managers now feel that staff development is an important part of their management job (with help from the Training Department, if required). Off-job courses are still justifiably popular but are only one of the methods that can be employed in helping staff to develop. On-job development can be used and controlled by the line manager. Delegation is one very powerful way of providing on-job development.

'Development' is a word that seems to be most often applied to the needs of someone who wants to progress within the organisation, i.e. to help them gain the skills and knowledge necessary for the next level upwards. Whilst delegation is a terrific way of helping them to gain experience of the next level in a controlled way, it can also be used to help someone to develop **within the job that they currently do**, and these people are likely to be the bulk of your team. Not everyone is capable of, or wants, promotion. Strangely enough, relatively few managers seem to see the potential for delegation in this light.

Identifying the needs

Look at any data you may have concerning the training and development needs of the people in your team. If your organisation uses an appraisal system, there is usually a section on training and development needs. Think about the tasks that you do and ask yourself whether delegating any of them would fill the needs of any of your people.

Delegating to help development towards the next level, i.e. potential promotion

From the needs you have identified above, you will know the skills and knowledge the person needs to gain in order to succeed at the next level. It can be a worthwhile activity to sit down with the person concerned and **jointly** produce the plan to meet the needs. They need your help and support throughout the entire development process so you might as well start as you intend to continue.

63

Development Plan for		Date:	
Skill/Knowledge area:	Actions:	Deadline:	Results:
1.			
2.			
3.			
4.			
5.			
6.			

Fig 6.1 Format for a Development Plan

Consider tasks that you currently do which, if delegated, would help them to fill these skill or knowledge gaps. A basic rule here is to 'start simple'. If a person needs to develop, say, presentation skills, don't put them in front of your largest customer first time out. You might think this is obvious, but it happens, honestly!

The 'Building Block' Approach

Old proverb goes ... 'If you want to eat an elephant, cut it up!'

The 'building block' approach breaks a new task down into 'bite-sized chunks', each one building on the next, until by the end, the person has dealt with the entire 'elephant'. An example might help to illustrate. Suppose someone needs to learn to prepare and make internal presentations to managers, and they have never made presentations before. The discussion may well result in a plan like this.

Plan

Objective: To develop the ability to prepare and make an effective presentation to managers within six months. (Criteria have been agreed in order to adequately measure 'effective'!)

Stage 1 Presentation to colleagues.

- Prepare: decide specific objective, and content to suit audience, draft outline and visual aids, review with manager, finalise outline and materials.

- Dummy run in private to manager, make any changes necessary.

- Make the ten-minute presentation at the meeting in June, encourage questions for group, ask for feedback from group, private review with manager after.

Stage 2 Presentation to managers.

- Accompany manager to a management meeting in July to see how presentations to managers differ. Discuss differences with manager afterwards.

- Prepare and make a presentation (including a question session) on behalf of the manager, to this management group (on a topic to be agreed with manager) in September. Dummy runs or reviews available as requested by the team member.

As you can see, the difficulty level increases but so to does the level of individual responsibility for 'calling the shots'.

This brings us on to another key principle:

> **Expect, and *allow for*, some minor mistakes**

Delegation is often a learning situation. When anyone undertakes a new task, they are bound to make some mistakes. However, the other side is that nobody wants a disaster. The controls/reviews should prevent potential disasters but what should be done about potential or actual *minor* mistakes?

Potential minor mistakes
If you spot a potential minor mistake, it is natural to raise it and so prevent it. However if the person's plan has this minor flaw, it may be better to let them make the mistake (it is after all their plan) then help them to learn from it. As it is only minor, it is unlikely to have a dramatically adverse effect on the objective. Whether you prevent a minor mistake or let it happen depends on the person. A team member who is lacking confidence might be very upset by making even a minor mistake whereas someone who thinks that they know it all may well learn something important from making it. Only you can decide what is appropriate for the individual concerned.

65

Actual minor mistakes
The important thing here is for the manager to be supportive. Try to give the impression that you are not expecting perfection; minor mistakes are normal. You are concerned less about the actual mistake and more about what the person did having made it, and consequently, what they learned for the future. If it is you, rather than the team member, who spots the mistake, you will need to explain why you feel it is a mistake and ask them what they would do to correct it. 'This report's a load of junk! I wish I had never given you the job to do', doesn't help too much.

Consider delegating some of your bigger decisions

Promotions are usually accompanied by increased responsibility and authority. So giving a person a chance to make some decisions at a higher level is a real aid to their development. The person needs to be competent at the smaller decisions first (the 'building block' approach again) but once this stage is adequately reached, then you may well consider stretching them with a bigger decision, providing they feel ready for the responsibility that goes with it. It may well help to position the first big decision as the need to prepare a recommendation to you. Then, if they have shown that they can handle it effectively, you may let them actually make the final decision on the second occasion, reviewing it with you before they implement it. If that works, then they are on their own with the third decision, simply informing you of what they have done. This 'building block' approach lets them develop but, under control. You always have that nagging fear of impending doom, but the building blocks should have reduced the likelihood of 'doom' to a minimum.

If you have ever taught a child to ride a bike, you will know that you charge along behind them holding the saddle, with them pedalling like mad. Once you are happy that they can keep their balance and won't bump into the nearest tree (or you are too puffed to go on), you let go and hope that you have not done so too early. They might be somewhat wobbly but they usually stay upright. Delegation for development is pretty much like that.

Delegating to help development within the current job

Not everyone wants or is capable of promotion. Some are happy doing what they are doing, but that does not mean that you cannot use delegation to help them develop. Everyone is capable of improving their performance, even if only a little. Suppose a team member has to manage a section budget as part of his normal role but feels that he could be doing a much better job on it. His budget management is adequate but could be even better. You could counsel him regarding the specific improvements he could make, or you could delegate some work related to your departmental budget that would help him to learn more advanced aspects of managing a budget 'under your wing' and help him to understand how his section budget fits in to the broader picture. He gets ideas to help him make his budget management even better and you get help with some of your work.

Again a discussion is worthwhile and you might like to use a modified version of the joint plan illustrated earlier.

A word of caution:

> **Beware of the phrase . . .**
>
> 'This job will be *good for your development*!'

Many people say it and actually **mean** it, but some most definitely DO NOT.

Some managers seem to use it as a way of 'dressing up' an otherwise boring, uninteresting job; trying to indicate that this is all part of some grand plan. People are not that gullible. The truth is valuable here. If you are going to delegate a task that has to be done but is boring and uninteresting, be honest with the person. Explain why you need their help, and apologise for the boring nature of it, if you like. If, most of the time, you try to give them rather more interesting tasks to do, they will understand that life cannot always be like that and get on and help you. They probably won't enjoy doing it, but at least they didn't have 'enjoyment' as an expectation.

TASKS THAT MOTIVATE

Firstly, it is worth considering what is meant by this word 'motivation'. We see motivation as encouraging someone to give their very best within their capabilities. It is worth remembering that motivation can be positive (based on encouragement) or negative (based often on threat). Our definition falls into the first category; the use of fear falls squarely into the second.

67

Most people enjoy interesting work so they are probably motivated when doing it (enjoyment and motivation do seem to run together). When considering which tasks to delegate for motivational purposes, decide what specific result you want. Not just in terms of the task itself but with regard to the effect that doing it will have on the person. Choose a task that will address the specific motivational issue that you are trying to handle. Be careful that you do not simply pick a task that you would have found enjoyable, at that stage. They may be different so discuss it with them and choose it together.

The 'My job is boring' syndrome

Has one of your team ever said this to you? It has to be said that some jobs, or at least aspects of it, *are* boring. This complaint is far from uncommon and, if you have encountered it, you may well have sat for some time trying to puzzle out what you can do to add a bit of interest. Whilst staff motivation is part of the job of a manager, it cannot all be one-way. It is their job and their working life too. There is a *shared* responsibility.

Consider asking them what *they* think can be done to help increase the interest. They, like you, might not be able to think of anything with regard to their own job. However, they may well feel that some aspect of your job could be extremely interesting and this could indicate possible tasks to delegate to aid their motivation. What might seem like boring routine to you might be extremely interesting to them because they simply have no experience of it.

An engineering apprentice was given the job of producing 5000 pins on an automatic lathe; basically put metal rods in one end and take out the finished pins at the other. Not exactly equivalent to composing Beethoven's Ninth! He was bored but stuck at it. The charge hand on that section recognised this but left him alone for a day. Half-way through day two, the apprentice was going ever so slightly daft with boredom and at just the right moment, over came the charge hand. *'You're doing well with those, John. When you have finished them tomorrow, I'll let you set the lathe up for another job which another apprentice can do. You'll have done your stint. Good lad'.* Setting up the machine was part of that particular charge hand's job and he had probably done that straightforward set-up a hundred times before so it was routine for him. However he knew that the apprentice had not done it and would enjoy trying it. Imagine the motivational state of the apprentice for the remainder of the job. What he was doing was appreciated and he had something to look forward to, after the boring bit.

> **Your 'routine' can be someone else's 'challenge and interest'**

Consider tasks that you are skilled at doing

People usually like to extend their skills and knowledge as we said in an earlier section. If you consider delegating some of these tasks, it may well represent a significant challenge to a team member. It is also likely to result in a real sense of achievement if the person learns to make a good job of it and receive justified praise from you. That will really mean something as they probably already know that you are particularly good at whatever it is.

There are two difficulties for *you* here though. Firstly, if you are good at it, you probably enjoy doing it so you need to convince yourself of the need to 'let go', occasionally at least (do you remember the earlier section on 'jobs we enjoy doing'?) Secondly, there is 'ego' to contend with. *Suppose that they do it as well as, or even better, than me?* Really, that's got to be a benefit! Now there are two people in the team who can handle it well. Having said that, it is fairly unlikely, in the short term at least, that they will be as good as you. You already have the skills born of experience. They may just be a natural but they are rare. It takes most people a while to become really skilled. To give an example of the power of this, a tale of a secretary/PA and her boss.

The manager was extremely skilled at dealing with customers face to face. His secretary had only very limited experience of this, but was very good with people generally. The organisation was exhibiting at a Trade Fair and on one of the days, the manager had a prior appointment so could not be on the stand. One of the directors suggested that he might consider asking his secretary to stand in for him, and he was totally in agreement. The secretary was understandably apprehensive at first but it was decided that she should attend an earlier day at the Trade Fair to 'get the feel of it'. This went well, with help/guidance as needed; she then stood in for the manager. Motivation was high; a challenging task but one that was realistic. One of the customers she met on her day even took the trouble to phone the manager to say how impressed he was with the way he was treated.

69

Our ability to do a particular task very well can be passed on with the right form of coaching, and the result can be highly motivational.

TASKS THAT ENABLE 'BETTER' DECISIONS BY USING THE GREATER SKILLS OR KNOWLEDGE OF YOUR PEOPLE

In the previous section, we considered jobs at which you are highly skilled. This section considers the reverse of that. There may be tasks you do that could be better accomplished by a member of your team. Resulting in motivation for them, and in 'better' decisions.

Look closely at the tasks you carry out regularly and ask yourself whether there is anyone in the team who could do any of them more effectively than you. To use ourselves as an example for once, this tale concerns artistic skills, or lack of them.

Shirley is a Partner in the business, so does not report to me, but this story will still illustrate the principle. When working at home, my role involves the development of training course materials, i.e. exercises, handouts, overhead transparencies, etc. Shirley handles the bulk of the administrative work. My artistic skills are roughly equivalent to those of a three-year-old (my boats look like cars). In fact, thinking about it, most three-year-olds are better than me! Prior to Shirley joining me in the business, all my transparencies were 'text only' unless I could find some drawing that I could copy or trace. Shirley is however a superb artist and has improved the transparencies beyond recognition. Many now have cartoons or pictures that get the message over so much better. Shirley enjoys doing it and I get the benefit of overhead transparencies that are vastly more interesting. Technically, transparencies are part of my job but I am happy to 'delegate' them to someone with far better skills.

 If you have the opportunity to delegate, list below any of your tasks which, if delegated, would help you

- make better use of your time
- develop people in your team
- motivate people in your team
- enable 'better' decisions by using the abilities of people in your team.

70

SUMMARY – CHAPTER 6

Objective Setting

Set the objectives at the right level

An effective objective should:

- be RESULT-oriented, rather than activity-oriented

- be clear, measurable (if possible), and realistic

- show the result expected, the deadline and any constraints

Deciding which Tasks to delegate

Those tasks which:

- help you to make better use of your time

- develop members of your team

- help you motivate people in the team

- enable 'better' decisions, by allowing you more time for your major decisions, and by using the abilities of your team.

KEY POINTS TO REMEMBER

- 'What am I here for?'

- Don't confuse 'urgent' with 'important'

- Your 'routine' tasks can be interesting to others

- The 'Ostrich' approach – hoping the danger might go away

- Staff development is an important part of your job as a manager

- Delegate using the 'building block' approach

- Accept minor mistakes; they are inevitable, with delegated work

- Involve the person to help identify 'interesting work'

- Accept that some people in your team may do some things better than you. Be grateful for it!

Choosing the right person

Overview of this chapter

In the previous chapter, we identified possible **tasks** that can be suitable for delegation. In this chapter, we will look at the issues surrounding the question of how to go about choosing the right **person** to carry out the delegated task.

The difficulty here is that, rather than choose a person for a task, you may occasionally want to choose a task for a particular individual, i.e. for development, so there can be something of a 'chicken or egg' situation. Whichever way round it is, you need to know the **requirements of the task** and the **abilities of the people**. Both will be covered in this chapter.

What are the objectives for this chapter?

When you have read this chapter, you should:

- know how to identify the requirements of a particular task suitable for delegation
- know how to evaluate and record the skills and knowledge of the people in your team, to enable you to select the person most suited to carry out the task
- know how to decide the appropriate level of delegation (the extent to which you 'let go') to suit the task and the person.

What is covered in this chapter?

- What does the task need?
- How do you choose the right (most suitable) person?
- Recording the information on the task and the people; an example and a blank form

- Deciding the extent to which you can 'let go.'
- Delegating sideways or upwards.

What does the task need?

In order to decide the right person for a particular task that you want to delegate, you need to know what you are looking for. The first step has to be to identify what skills and knowledge the task requires, for successful completion. The main difficulty here is knowing how far to go in breaking the job down; too little and the requirements are still unclear, too much and it becomes too complicated to be of use. The trick, if there is one, is to find a happy medium that gives sufficient detail to help your choice of person, without the need to spend three days trying to analyse every aspect of the job in fine detail.

The task needs to be broken down into **skill and knowledge requirements**. If you already delegate, you probably do this to some extent at least. For many managers this is virtually 'unconscious thinking'. For example, 'I can't give this to David. He won't cope', or 'Pam can handle this one. She has done similar things before'. Criteria are there, but at the back of your mind. This section looks at how to make these criteria rather more **visible**.

We can provide some thoughts regarding possible skill requirements, but knowledge requirements vary enormously depending very much on the specific task and situation, so we can only generalise here.

AN OPTIONAL APPROACH TO THE ACTIVITIES THAT FOLLOW

At the end of the section entitled 'Recording the information' later in this chapter, we have included a blank Delegation form that you might like to use to record the skills and knowledge for your own tasks and people. To help you to decide whether you like this layout, you can use it as you work through any of the following activities, if you wish, rather than use the space allowed in the text. It is up to you.

THE SKILL REQUIREMENTS OF THE TASK

Let's start by defining what we mean by a 'skill'. To us it means 'competence, ability, or aptitude in a particular area of activity, i.e. communication'.

Identify an important, but straightforward task that you do regularly. Note below (or on the form later in this chapter) the skills that you believe are required to complete the job successfully.

Task:

_____

_____

Skills required:

_____

_____

_____

_____

_____

_____

75

_____

_____

_____

_____

_____

_____

_____

_____

_____

_____

_____

_____

What follows is a list of possible skills for which there may be a requirement in any task. Remember from what was said earlier that this is not an exhaustive list of skills, but what we believe to be a 'happy medium'. You may prefer more or less detail. That's fine; you can simplify them or add to them as you wish. The aim here is to provide a working list of skills, with definitions, that will at least get you started. Think of them as a checklist; it is unlikely that any task will require **all** of these skills.

If you believe that a task *does* require all of the skills on your list, please challenge your thinking. Make sure this really is the case as you are likely to need the Archangel Gabriel to complete it successfully, and he is probably otherwise engaged.

How do you actually *identify* the skills required?

Some people find it relatively easy to do, whilst others find it extremely hard, e.g. 'I'm not sure. You just need to be able to . . . sort of . . . do the job.' If you are finding this difficult, start by breaking down the job you identified earlier into its component parts (key tasks). Then take each key task and look through the list of skills to see if any of them are necessary **to complete that part**. The question you need to be asking is: What does he or she need to be able to actually *do* in order to complete this part of the job?'. Dealing with it in this way seems to make it somewhat easier, and practice helps. If you are still stuck, look at the example of the completed Delegation form in the section 'Recording the information' later in this chapter, which identifies the skills that we believe are involved in running a meeting. (See Figure 7.1 opposite).

Rating the skills required

Several different skills may be needed but it is unlikely that they will all require the same level of proficiency. Rating the skills in terms of the proficiency necessary for successful completion of the task can be very useful when you come to decide who best could undertake the task for you. Again, we have tried to keep the rating scale simple so that you can use it quickly.

For practice, you might like to try these ratings on the skills you identified in the previous activity (see Figure 7.2 overleaf).

THE KNOWLEDGE REQUIREMENTS OF THE TASK

We define 'knowledge' as 'having specific information about a subject'. As we have said, the knowledge requirements depend very much on

Personal skills	
Numeracy	the ability to handle numbers, i.e. arithmetic
Verbal communication	the ability to be clear, concise, and tactful when speaking to people face to face or by phone, and to listen effectively
Written communication	the ability to produce clear, concise reports, letters, or memos
Information extraction	the ability to accurately identify key issues/data from conversations or written material
Negotiation/Persuasion	the ability to negotiate/persuade via well-presented facts, and obtain agreement and commitment
Personal planning and control	the ability to set clear objectives for self; plan, prioritise, and control the plan and time to ensure that the desired result is achieved
Creativity	the ability to generate new ideas and approaches
Decision making/problem solving	the ability to make effective, timely decisions, and find/correct the causes of problems
Management skills	
Organising others	the ability to establish objectives/duties for others, and ensure adequate communication between the people involved
Leadership/motivation	the ability to use the right approach for the particular situation, and to encourage in people a willingness to give their best
Coaching/counselling	the ability to help people to improve their performance
Delegation	the ability to entrust part of their job to another person and achieve a successful outcome
Risk taking	the ability to take calculated risks and use judgement when necessary, i.e. when information is missing but a decision must be made and being prepared to take responsibility for it

Fig 7.1 Possible personal and management skills

H = HIGH	■ This skill is vital for success
	■ Person selected needs to be proficient in all aspects of this skill, and must have successfuly demonstrated full use of this skill previously on a task of comparable level
M = MEDIUM	■ Aspects of this skill are necessary, but not vital
	■ Person selected needs to be proficient in only some aspects of this skill and some experience of using this skill on tasks at a lower level would be helpful
L = LOW	■ Aspects of this skill will be helpful
	■ Person needs the ability to develop these aspects, but no prior experience of using this skill is needed
LEFT BLANK	■ This skill is not needed for successful completion of the task

Fig 7.2 Ratings scale and definitions for skills required

the specific task and the situation. Having said that, there are some broad areas that you might consider:

■ **Procedural**, e.g. knowledge of company policies and procedures
■ **Managerial**, e.g. how to organise a meeting
■ **Technical**, e.g. how to write a computer
■ **Financial**, e.g. how to prepare a budget
■ **Legal,** e.g. employment legislation

 The general list above cannot cover every possible aspect of knowledge. It might help you to make a note below (or on the blank form at the end of this chapter) of any **other** knowledge areas that you believe would be important for the type of work that you might delegate.

Now list (here, or on the form) the knowledge requirements for the task that you identified earlier (key points are sufficient).

_____

_____

_____

_____

_____

_____

_____

_____

How do you identify the knowledge requirements?

As with skills, some people find that identifying the knowledge requirements is easy; others find it difficult. An example might help. Think about the knowledge requirements for a taxicab driver. He or she would probably need to know

- the procedure for picking up customers and obtaining payment
- how to use a radio to keep in touch with their base
- motoring law – general, and as applied to cabs
- the geographical area in which they work
- possibly some understanding of how a car works; to handle minor maintenance (oil, water, etc.)

Rating scale for knowledge requirements

As with skills, several areas of knowledge may be needed but it is unlikely that they will all require the same depth of understanding. Rating the knowledge in terms of the depth of understanding necessary for successful completion of the task can be very useful when you come to decide who best could undertake the task for you. Again, we have tried to keep the rating scale simple so that you can use it quickly (see Figure 7.3 overleaf).

For practice, you might like to try these ratings out on the knowledge areas that you identified in the previous activity.

H = HIGH	■ Detailed knowledge is vital for success
	■ Person selected needs to have a full understanding of this entire knowledge area, and have prior experience in using that knowledge effectively on a task of comparable level
M = MEDIUM	■ Some knowledge is required, but not vital
	■ Person selected needs knowledge of some aspects of this area and some experience of using that knowledge on tasks at a lower level would be helpful
L = LOW	■ knowledge of the basics would be helpful
	■ Person selected needs to understand a few key factors, but no prior experience of using this knowledge is necessary
LEFT BLANK	■ No knowledge of this area is needed

Fig 7.3 Ratings scale and definitions for knowledge required

How do you choose the right (most suitable) person to carry out the delegated task?

In order to choose the most suitable person, (or to select a suitable task for a particular individual), it is important to evaluate the skills and knowledge that the people in your team possess. Having done that, it should then be possible to compare the skills and knowledge possessed by the individual, with those required to successfully complete the task.

HOW DO YOU ACTUALLY IDENTIFY THE SKILLS OR KNOWLEDGE THAT YOUR PEOPLE POSSESS?

If your organisation uses an appraisal system, look at the recent appraisals on your people. Many appraisal systems provide guidance on defining and measuring skills and knowledge, and you may well find that much of this work has been done already. Use the information from these appraisals/training plans to help you enter the information regarding each person in your team. Place it in the blank form in the section 'Recording the Information'.

'But we don't have an appraisal system, so what do I do?'

In which case, you need to start from 'scratch'. Start by considering the skills and knowledge needed in order to do their current job in your team. It is very easy to take a high level of skill or knowledge for granted, until you really start to think about it. Think about any 'performance' type discussions you have had with members of your team, and try to identify the level of skills or knowledge for each person. Having done this, there are likely to be some gaps where you are simply unsure. If there are only one or two gaps in each case, try to cover the areas concerned on the next occasion that you have a discussion. If there are a lot of gaps, you really have two options; fill in the information over a period of time, dealing with one or two gaps at each meeting, or have a single meeting with each person and deal with all of the gaps in one go. As a personal view, we would favour the latter option because the sooner you collect the information, the sooner you can start to use it to help you to plan what to delegate and to whom.

81

RATING SCALES FOR THE SKILLS AND KNOWLEDGE POS-SESSED BY INDIVIDUALS IN YOUR TEAM

The two rating scales used earlier (for the skills and knowledge required to successfully complete the task) have been designed so that you can use them here, with a slight modification, and so avoid the need for two separate scales for the task or the person. All that you need to do when using them for people is to read 'is or has' in place of 'needs'. When using the 'left blank' rating, this means that the person does not currently have that skill or knowledge. We believe that this is easier than using two separate sets of rating scales. It might seem complicated at first, but you will soon get used to doing this.

Using the form to highlight training or development needs

So far we have only talked about rating an individual's *present* level of skill or knowledge. Training and development needs can also be easily shown by putting a circle around the rating. See the example form under 'Recording the information' later in this chapter. 'But what about those areas you have left blank because the person does not have that skill or knowledge?' you may ask. Just put a circle in that box. It tells you that they have not *currently* got that skill or knowledge but **need to develop it**.

MAKING THE CHOICE

You now have the information concerning the requirements of the task that you want to delegate, and information of the skills and knowledge of your people.

When you need the task completed quickly and effectively, look for the person in your team whose skills and knowledge most closely matches the requirements of the task. If they are not available, because of other commitments, look for the next closest match, and so on.

If the task is not urgent, consider whether you could use the opportunity to train someone who needs to develop skills or knowledge that would be covered by this task. The lack of urgency not only takes the pressure off them when they are doing the job, but also helps you should you need to spend time guiding them.

Where your objective is to train or develop an individual, try to find a task that would provide the skills or knowledge that they need. Remember not to try to do too much in one go (remember the elephant?). Try to aim at one skill or body of knowledge at a time otherwise there is the danger of putting the person into 'overload'.

Recording the information

This section contains two versions of the form discussed earlier in the chapter.

- an example of a completed Delegation form
- a blank version of the form that you might care to use.

AN EXAMPLE OF A COMPLETED DELEGATION FORM

An example might well be of use to illustrate the ideas we have suggested in this chapter; a picture tells a thousand words, etc.

The Background:

The manager has a team of four people and needs to delegate the task of running a departmental meeting to agree the sales targets for next month to one of his team as he will absent from the office at the time set for the meeting.

The team comprises of David (the deputy), Jane (an experienced salesperson), Leroy (fairly new salesperson), and Martha (just completed her initial sales training).

DELEGATION					
Task: Run the monthly sales meeting on 25 July next to agree sales targets by area for August					
Date: 23 June					

Skill	Task Require-ments	David (deputy)	Jane (5 yrs in sales)	Leroy (8 mths in sales)	Martha (just completed training)
Numeracy	**M**	M	H	L	M
Verbal communication	**H**	H	H	M	M
Written communication	**L**	(L)	H	M	(L)
Information extraction	**H**	M	(L)		
Negotiation persuasion	**H**	H	M	M	(L)
Personal planning and control	**M**	M	(L)	H	M
Creativity		H	M	L	H
Decision-making/ problem solving	**H**	(M)	M	(L)	( )
Management Skills					
Organising others	**H**	M	(L)		
Leadership/ motivation	**H**	H	(L)		

Fig 7.4 Example of completed Delegation Form

83

Skill	Task Require- ments	David (deputy)	Jane (5 yrs in sales)	Leroy (8 mths in sales)	Martha (just completed training)
Coaching/ counselling		(L)			
Delegation		(L)			
Knowledge					
Sales performance to date by area	**H**	H	H		
Company procedure for meetings	**M**	(L)			

Fig 7.4 Continued

For practice, if you wish, identify the training/development needs, and consider possible actions, for each of the four people in this example:

_____

_____

_____

_____

_____

_____

_____

_____

_____

_____

_____

This is a hypothetical example so you probably had many 'ifs and buts,' but there are some general issues that you should have identified and handled in some way. Our broad analysis follows. Compare it with yours to see if there are any key needs/issues that you have missed. Do NOT worry if your actions differ from our ideas. There are numerous ways of handling these needs, but ask yourself whether the action you proposed would really meet the need. For example, there is no point sending Martha for training, as she has *been* trained and is presumably sufficiently competent to start selling. The need probably is to help her **develop** her low level of skill 'in the field'.

David

David (the deputy) is probably the best person for this delegated task, (but see the note regarding Jane).

Most of the needs identified are probably aimed at development towards the next level (you might say he is virtually ready for promotion). His written communication skills are low and will probably be more important at the next level, so he could be asked to produce a report on the meeting. A briefing by David's manager prior to running this meeting should help David improve his knowledge of the company meetings' procedure. Decision-making and/or problem-solving need some improvement prior to, or soon after promotion, so the meeting briefing could include a discussion on ways that David might develop his skills in the meeting.

David has no experience or skill in delegation or coaching/counselling and both would be important at the next level. Another task or tasks would be needed to help him here.

Jane

Jane is a very experienced salesperson. Personal planning and information extraction are both low. A task that is complicated, with buried key information, yet requires planning to avoid it going on and on would probably help Jane. Jane has needs identified in the management skills area so, in the longer term, is probably looking for promotion or increased responsibility. Relatively low level management tasks could be found to help her with organising and leadership, e.g. act as project leader on a fairly straightforward project.

If David was unable to run the meeting, it *might* be possible to delegate it to Jane, if her leadership/organising skills are sufficient for this internal meeting. This could be asking too much at this stage.

Leroy

Leroy is fairly new to the department. The only area with which he needs help, at this point, is on his decision-making/problem-solving. He may need some form of training to help him learn the basics, followed by some opportunity on-job to practise what he has learned on a relatively simple, low risk task (perhaps coached by David?).

Martha

Martha is brand new to the department having just completed her initial training in sales. As her 'manager', we would not consider delegating any of *our* tasks to her at the moment. In the future though, her high level of creativity could be a real asset in considering tasks to delegate. Considering her role, we would concentrate on the need to improve negotiation/persuasion at this point (possibly coached by Jane 'in the field'?)

There is a need to develop decision-making/problem-solving skill (it is not there at the moment) and to improve written communications (again David might give her a straightforward decision-making task and ask for a report on it).

A BLANK VERSION OF THE FORM

This blank version is similar to the example used earlier. The only differences are that the main knowledge areas are included and blank lines added to enable you to add skills or knowledge required in your situation that we have not covered.

There are two ways to use the form:

- copy the format and enter data by hand
- produce it on a word processor.

Copy the format and enter data by hand

This is probably the simplest method. Hand write a master that suits you and your situation then copy it as required. The problem is that, over a period of time, the information regarding the skills and knowledge of your people changes as needs are met and new needs arise. Forms produced in this way tend to have a considerable number of alterations, especially if the task is fairly long-term, and tend to become 'messy'.

Produce the form on a word processor

This method is more time consuming initially than the hand-written version. It is best to put the basic skill and knowledge ratings for your people on to the master. Once this master is produced, it is very easy to produce copies for other tasks, and very easy to update as the skills and knowledge needs are met. This updated information is automatically there when you produce a new copy for a new task.

DELEGATION					
Task:					
Date:					
Skill	**Task Require-ments**				
Numeracy					
Verbal communication					
Written communication					
Information extraction					
Negotiation persuasion					
Personal planning and control					
Creativity					
Decision-making/ problem-solving					

Fig 7.5 Suggested form for recording skills and knowledge

87

Skill	Task Require-ments				
Management Skills					
Organising others					
Leadership/ motivation					
Coaching/ counselling					
Delegation					
Knowledge					
Procedural					
Managerial					
Technical					
Financial					
Legal					

Fig 7.5 Continued

Deciding the extent to which you can 'let go'

You have, by now, selected the person to carry out the task, or have picked a task that will help train/develop an individual in the team. The next question is, 'How far dare I "let go"?'

It all depends on the gap between the task requirements and their present skills and knowledge. If you try and teach your youngster to swim, you don't just throw them into the pool and hope they float, do you?

If it's their first time in the water, you might try to have some fun but you would hang on for dear life and try to build up their confidence. The next few times, as they became more confident, and are prepared to take their feet off the bottom of the pool, you might need to support them, less and less. Then, the big break-through; they can actually swim now. Only a few strokes but they are doing it on their own with you watching, ready to grab if need be. Gradually you let them go further and further away from you, until at last, you can get out of the pool.

In the early days, even though you might be sitting sunning yourself by the side of the pool, you still keep an eye on them, just in case they still need your help and encouragement. There is a close parallel between teaching your youngster to swim and delegating.

89

'IN THE SWIM!' (HOW FAR DO YOU 'LET GO'?)

Their experience	*Your involvement*
None	**Let 'em have fun, but hang on!**
Low – know basics	**Support them on important things**
Reasonably experienced	**Let them decide the support they need. As ability develops, get out of the pool, but watch**
Fully experienced (As much as, or even greater than yours)	**On their own now, tell you the outcome**

THE 'LEVELS' OF DELEGATION

Expanding on the bullet points shown in the figure 'In the swim'.

Level 1 No experience
- They have no experience of the task as yet.
- They have the ability, and desire, to learn the basics.
- They are unable to do it alone, so there is frequent monitoring by you.
- They do it with you, and may even do some of the detailed work for you.

Level 2 Know the basics
- They have only limited experience, but know the basics.
- They have the ability and desire to learn more than the basics.
- They do the important things with you; the rest on their own with control checkpoints set by you.

Level 3 Reasonably experienced
- They are reasonably experienced, but might still need occasional guidance.
- They have the ability and desire to learn the advanced aspects of the task.
- At this level, let them decide what help they need from you, and let them set the checkpoints. This may include a request to review major decisions with you before implementation.

Level 4 Fully experienced
- Their experience/ability is as good as, (or even greater than), your own.
- They feel able to handle the entire task and are prepared to take responsibility for the decisions.

Now you can 'let go': review and agree the overall objective (including any constraints) with them, check that they still feel able to handle it, *let them get on with it*, and advise you of their decisions and the outcome *after the event*.

Note: You might think that delegating at this level equals 'abdication'. It does not! Whilst you have justifiably given them the authority for day-to-day control and to make independent decisions, overall control is still there by virtue of the constraints that you included in the objective, e.g. Do 'x' within a budget of £3000 by a certain date.

Few people seem to have the courage to delegate at Level 4. If you already delegate to this level, full marks to you; you are fairly rare. Like any management activity, it has risks but they are **calculated** risks, based on your judgement of the task and the person. If you have chosen the right person to operate at this level, the risks are minimised, and the potential motivational and developmental effects of success are phenomenal.

If you have the opportunity to delegate already, are there any tasks that could be delegated at a higher level?

If you are not yet able to delegate, are there any tasks delegated to you that you could handle at a higher level? If so, try discussing them with your manager.

SOME POTENTIAL TRAPS WHEN TRYING TO SELECT THE PERSON FOR THE TASK

There are a couple of traps into which even experienced managers can unwittingly fall.

The 'No experience' trap

If someone has never done a particular task before, there seems to be some unwritten management law that says, 'No experience = no ability'. This thinking can mean you are not even considering a very useful potential source of help.

They may not have done it before but they may well have what it takes to LEARN to do it with your help. If they lack any experience all you need ask is, 'Do they have the ability to learn it, and the desire to do it?'. If the answer is 'yes' and there is enough time available, this could be the ideal opportunity to help them develop some experience, together with the skills and knowledge that go with that experience.

The 'This will be a challenge' trap

This goes something like 'Karen will enjoy having a go at this; she will see it as a real challenge. When I was doing her job, I would have loved to try it'. Have you ever thought something like that?

Let's look at this situation, which seems to hold true for many people. Most of us try to do as good a job as we can, then along comes someone who says, 'You have been doing a grand job as a computer programmer (or whatever) for the last four years. We have decided to promote you to Team Leader next Monday'. (We will leave aside the issue of whether anyone has thought to give you any training for this new role.)

Many organisations seem to have another unwritten rule that goes, 'To be promoted, you must be pretty good in your current job'. The rationale appears to be that successful people already have 'street credibility' that will help them to establish themselves as managers more quickly. Everyone knows that the best salespeople don't necessarily make the best sales managers. However, if you were Sales Director, would you *really* promote a person who was a terrible salesperson to manage a sales team, even if they displayed some of the management skills?

Now, if you were promoted because you were good in your previous role, and could handle a management role at the next level, there is a trap. When deciding who should be chosen to carry out a delegated task, we often seem to ask ourselves how *we* would have felt about doing it. If we were in the top 10 per cent before, it is a pointless question unless the person you are considering also falls into that category. Often we are considering giving the job to a person somewhere in the other 90 per cent. So what you (and perhaps others in the top 10 per cent) might view as a **challenge**, could be seen by the rest as an **impossibility**. Suppose that in your old role it would have taken you a day to assemble a presentation for the Board on behalf of your old boss, so you think that is a reasonable deadline. It is probably only a reasonable 'challenge' for the experienced; less experienced people would perhaps need three days to do it and so would view it as an impossibility.

As you know, there is a vast motivational difference between challenge and impossibility. Probably, in the past, you have been given what you judged to be an impossible (not challenging) task. Think about how you felt. The important thing to remember is not how YOU would view it but how *they* would see it. Think about their likely reaction when you offer them the task.

There is an additional point to consider though. Some people might genuinely believe that the task is impossible, because they just lack confidence in themselves. (It doesn't help matters to say, 'Oh. I know you will cope'. They don't believe you.) You may be able to instil that confidence if you have some **factual evidence** that they could handle it; for example, where they have successfully completed a different task that requires the same skills or knowledge. They may not have recognised the parallel. If you believe that you can prove to them that they CAN cope, then you can select them. Beware of 'railroading' them though.

Delegating sideways or upwards

Throughout this chapter, we have concentrated on selecting the most suitable person *in your team* because this is by far the most typical source of help. It is important to remember that you could also ask another manager to help you by taking on the task, or you might ask your own boss. Every situation must be considered in its own right but this form of delegation may be appropriate when:

(a) you have a new or very inexperienced team and a fairly advanced job to delegate, e.g. running an important client meeting that cannot be moved, when nobody in your team has ever run a meeting before.

(b) there is a major priority clash, e.g. a genuine crisis has arisen on which you must act, there is nobody available in your team to handle another urgent and important job for you, and a colleague manager could help,

(c) it would be unreasonable to expect a team member to handle the task in your absence, e.g. the Board insist that your departmental budget must be cut immediately by 50 per cent. If an unpleasant task such as this must be done on a certain date and circumstances are such that you cannot do it or postpone it, your only option is to request help from your own boss. Note that you will need an extremely good reason to do this.

93

Remember that they are probably just as busy as you so ensure that your reasons for requesting their help are valid before you ask; not just because it is the 'easy option'. Secondly, it is also important to bear in mind that most managers (particularly your own manager) would be thinking, *What are you doing to develop your people so that one of your team can learn to handle this type of job in the future?*

SUMMARY – CHAPTER 7

- Identify the skills and knowledge needed to successfully complete the delegated task, and rate them to show importance

- Break the task down into 'key tasks' if it helps the analysis

- Identify the skills and knowledge of people in your team, and rate them to show present level (or desired level)

- Use the format of the form in the chapter to record and update information

- The levels of delegation

  Level 1 – Do it with you, help with detail, frequent monitoring

  Level 2 – They do important things with you, the rest on their own with checkpoints set by you

  Level 3 – They decide what help they need and set the checkpoints. They may want to review major decisions with you prior to implementation

  Level 4 – Full delegation; review objective (including constraints), with them. **Let them go**, advise you of decisions/ outcome after the event

- Two traps to avoid

  Assuming that no experience means no ability

  'This will be a challenge for you.' (challenge versus impossibility)

8

Handling the discussion

This may well be one of the first chapters that you might turn to if you already have some experience of delegating, and decided to read the book selectively. Consequently it might be of help to briefly summarise the key points from Chapters 3, 4, 5, 6, and 7 in order that you can check what should already have been considered by the time you reach this stage in delegation. If there are items there that you want to explore, go to the chapter and read through the relevant section before working through this chapter.

If you are systematically reading through the entire book, you can skip this summary unless you feel that it will be a useful element of revision at this point.

KEY POINTS PRECEDING CHAPTERS 3 TO 7

The following points should *already* have been considered

Chapters 3, 4, & 5 General points

- Whether you are delegating or assigning work
- Managers need a positive attitude towards delegation
- Others in the team may have greater knowledge/skill than you in certain areas of expertise (Be grateful !)
- The need to separate valid reasons for not delegating, from excuses (born out of fear often) in order to avoid it

Chapter 6 Deciding which *task* to delegate

- Ask yourself 'What am I here for?'
- Identify tasks which, if delegated, would:
  - help you make better use of your time
  - help you to develop people in your team
  - help you to motivate people
  - enable 'better' decisions

- Set a result-oriented objective that is clear, measurable and realistic
- Don't confuse 'important' with 'urgent'
- Use the 'building block' approach when delegating

Chapter 7 Choosing the most suitable *person*

- Identify the skills/knowledge required to complete the task successfully
- Identify the skills/knowledge of the people in your team
- Make a choice depending on the situation, i.e. speed, plenty of time, for development etc.
- Decide on the right level for delegation depending on their experience and ability.

Overview of this chapter

In this chapter we will look at the principles involved in preparing for and running the delegation discussion. The discussion itself is probably one of the most important aspects of the entire delegation process. Sadly, it is occasionally somewhat less than effective; not enough time or trouble is taken over it. Some managers even try to do it in 30 seconds flat whilst standing by the coffee machine!

What are the objectives for this chapter?

When you have read this chapter, you should:

- know how to prepare for the delegation discussion
- know how to run the discussion effectively.

What is covered in this chapter?

- Preparing to hold the delegation discussion.
- The discussion itself: analysis of a delegation discussion.
- Overview of the delegation discussion.
- Starting the discussion on the right foot.
- The main body of the discussion.
- Ending the discussion effectively.

Preparing to hold the delegation discussion

> **If you *fail to prepare*, then you *prepare to fail!***

This is a very old saying. We don't know who originally said it but it is very applicable in the delegation situation Unfortunately, some managers don't seem to do any preparation at all. 'I need this job done by tonight. Janet has just finished another job so I'll get her to do this one.' Then they wonder why things didn't go as perhaps they should.

WHAT YOU HAVE ALREADY DECIDED

When you reach the point where you want to actually prepare for your delegation discussion, you have probably decided:

- your objective (the result you want to achieve)
- the task that you will delegate
- the person to whom you will delegate
- the level to which you are prepared to delegate.

Note: If you are not sure how to go about any of the above steps, you may need to read Chapters 6 and/or 7 that cover these areas.

REVIEW THE OBJECTIVE

It may be some time since you thought about the objective for this delegation opportunity so it is worthwhile to review the objective and ensure that it is still appropriate for the current situation. If not, it is important to modify it now as it forms the keystone for all of the preparation that follows.

Check that the objective :

- clearly shows the **result** (convince the director), rather than an activity (make a presentation to the director)
- is **clear**, i.e. will be understood by the person to whom you intend to delegate the task
- is **measurable** (if possible), i.e. there are criteria by which you and the delegatee will be able to measure successful completion

97

- is **realistic**, i.e. within the capabilities of the delegatee in the time available
- includes the **deadline** for completion; (avoid 'as soon as possible')
- shows any **constraints**, i.e. limits on authority. For example, decide which computer to buy, within a cost limit of £1500 per machine (excluding software and printer).

CONSIDER THE BACKGROUND

The 'background' includes:

- why is this task being delegated?
- why are you choosing that person to do the task?
- what skills and knowledge are required to carry out the task successfully?
- what skills and knowledge does the person possess, (and identification of any gaps)?

98

Why is this task being delegated?

Ask yourself why you have selected this particular task to delegate. During the discussion, it will be important to make this clear to the person who is going to do the job for you, otherwise they will put their own interpretation on it. This can produce a situation where YOU think the job will help them to develop particular skills (but don't tell them that), whereas THEY might think that you are just 'dumping' a job that you can't be bothered to do. Not the most motivational atmosphere!

Why are you choosing that person to carry out the task for you?

As you know from Chapter 7, there could be numerous reasons for asking that particular person. Again, it is vital to be clear as to the reason, or they will simply put their own interpretation on your choice. This can result in somewhat different problems from those mentioned in the previous section regarding task.

If, for example, you ask one of your team to run a meeting for you because their 'chairing' skills are excellent; they on the other hand interpret that as you 'grooming them for stardom' as they want to progress in the organisation. They might not have actually told you this, but since when has that stopped any of us making assumptions.

They run the meeting well on your behalf but are not asked again (because you are there). They now wonder whether they did something wrong. Have they ruined their chances of promotion, etc.? It might sound a little like abject paranoia, but it is born out a lack of communication ON BOTH SIDES. It does not need to happen, and with adequate preparation, it should not!

What skills and knowledge are required to complete the task successfully?

Look back at your Delegation form for this task and remind yourself of

- the skills and level of proficiency needed and
- the knowledge and depth of understanding required.

If it is some while since you completed the form (the date should be on the form), consider whether there have been any significant changes in the task that would result in changes to the skills or knowledge required. If so, make the alterations now. This information will be needed during the next stage of your preparation so keep the form handy. The following example illustrates the importance of maintaining an up-to-date record of any changes that occur.

99

A manager in a medium-sized building firm had to produce a six-monthly stock usage report (to show how stocks of low usage items were moving). When the next report became due, the manager asked one of his team to compile the report and send it in as he himself would be on holiday on the due date. The team member asked to put the report together had done so a couple of times in the past so there seemed to be no problem. Whilst the manager was on holiday, the report was duly completed and sent. Back came the report with a note to the effect that it was unacceptable as the data now had to be input via a terminal to the Stock Control system. The team member who had produced the original rejected report had not used a terminal before. So he asked for some guidance, got help from a colleague who was used to terminals, and fed in the data. The whole process, including the wasted report, took around two days. Properly organised, it should have taken about four hours.

When the manager returned, he was asked about the change in procedure. With a look of horror on his face he said, *'Sorry. I forgot to tell you about that. They changed it just after the last one. It was a while ago now. Besides it could have waited until I got back.'*

If the manager had updated any skill/knowledge records for that task, perhaps he might not have forgotten. Even if he had, a glance at the form before delegating the task, would have revealed the need for terminal skills. Perhaps the job would have been given to someone with the necessary skills.

Although not directly related to keeping skills and knowledge information up to date, what about the last comment? Our reply would have been something like, 'Why did you give it to me then?' The team member had shown a bit of initiative believing that the information was important, and all he got for his trouble was, 'It could have waited'.

'Thanks for helping out' would have been nice, and justified. If you were that team member, how would you view the next delegated job from that manager?

What skills and knowledge does the person possess, (and identification of any gaps)?

Review your thoughts regarding the skills and knowledge possessed by the person to whom you intend to delegate. If it has been some time since the form was compiled, consider whether any of your ratings should now be changed. If changes are needed to bring the form up to date, verify that you still have the right task/person match.

If you are delegating to help someone develop, the plan can stretch over a fairly long period; one year is not uncommon. If there is a gap between preparation of the form and the event itself, it may be that the person has developed the skill or knowledge via other means in the interim period. Sometimes an unplanned opportunity just presents itself and you use it. Consequently, the original task might no longer be appropriate or necessary.

On the assumption that you are still going to proceed, compare the requirements of the task with the skills/knowledge of the person to identify any gaps. These gaps will be either STRENGTHS where the person's ability exceeds the requirement, or WEAKNESSES where the situation is reversed.

During the discussion, these strengths and weaknesses will be discussed with the intention of

- reinforcing the person's strengths, and showing how they relate to the task
- looking at weaknesses and identifying how carrying out the task will correct them

So it is vital that you are very clear on any gaps between task requirements and individual abilities.

REVIEW THE LEVEL OF DELEGATION TO ENSURE IT IS APPROPRIATE

This is the extent to which you 'let go', and was covered in Chapter 7. Basically there are four levels of control by you. The level chosen depends on the experience of the person selected to carry out the task. As a brief reminder the levels are:

Level	Their experience	Your involvement
1	None	Do the task with you. Frequent monitoring of any detailed work they do for you.
2	Know the basics	Support them on the important things. You set the checkpoints.
3	Reasonably experienced	Let them decide the help required & the check-points.
4	Fully experienced	Agree objective (and constraints), then let them go!

(If you want more detail about these levels and your involvement, please read the section in Chapter 7.)

As with skills and knowledge, if it is some time since you made the decisions concerning either the task, or the person who will carry it out, just review the level to ensure that it is still appropriate. This is particularly important if you have updated the skills and knowledge information. If the person's skill or knowledge has increased it may be that you need a lower level of control than you originally intended.

DECIDE CLEARLY THE AUTHORITY THEY NEED

'Authority' we have defined as 'the power to make independent decisions'. It is unlikely that you will delegate any authority at levels 1 or 2. At level 3, you may well delegate authority for some or all of the less important decisions, though you may both agree to review recommendations on the major decisions prior to implementation.

So it is important to be very clear as to which decisions are minor, and which are major. You may delegate authority for the minor decisions but not yet for the major ones. However, life being what it is, particular situations might not be quite so straightforward.

Suppose that the person to whom you intend to delegate the preparation of a presentation to a major customer may have only prepared two or three such presentations on your behalf in the past, so would probably be at level 3 in terms of experience. At this level, they may normally wish to review major decisions with you. In this particular case, imagine that the person has detailed knowledge of that particular major customer, knowing their likes and dislikes. The overall style of any presentation might well be seen as a major decision, but in this case the delegatee has more experience than you so could be given the authority for that particular 'major' decision.

The highest level of delegated authority usually exists at level 4. At this level, the person has the right to make independent decisions (within any constraints that you set) on all aspects of the delegated task without reference to you, and to notify you of the outcome after the event. They are really operating at your level so need the requisite authority, (and you need to trust them to use it sensibly).

Sometimes, word of mouth alone is not sufficient. An example might make this clear.

The Head of Personnel and Training in a large company had four middle managers reporting to him. He had a very significant budget and all major purchases (over £10,000) for Personnel and Training were under his direct control. On one occasion when he was on holiday, the opportunity to purchase a much needed piece of equipment (at a 30 per cent discount) came up. Although one of those managers was deputising, the financial system set limits for each manager (as departmental budget holders), and these had not been altered to accommodate the 'deputy' situation. Consequently, none of the four individual managers had sufficient authority to place the order, so the opportunity was lost. When the Head of Personnel and Training returned, the situation was discussed in order to prevent a recurrence. The senior manager promptly accepted that he had unintentionally slipped up, wrote to the Finance Director increasing the manager's cash limits when deputising, to match his own, and that was that.

Not only must the authority match the task, but the formal systems covering authority may also need to be updated.

CLEARLY IDENTIFY THE CONTROL CHECKPOINTS
(IN CASE THEY MISS ANY)

A 'checkpoint' is a progress or quality check prior to a critical step in the plan for the task. It alerts you to any problem **whilst there is still time to correct it.**

Checkpoints help you to:

- monitor (and, if necessary, influence) the progress of the task to ensure that the various important stages, and desired results are achieved to the right standard and at the right time

- discuss/review the major decisions (for levels other than level 4) prior to their implementation

- reassure the delegatee along the way, that things are 'going along satisfactorily'.

Decide what checkpoints are appropriate, considering the task and the person's level of knowledge and ability.

103

If you would like to practise identifying checkpoints, think about the following situation, decide those that you would set and note them below.

The situation

You are a Training Manager. Today is August and you are attending a five-day conference as from September next. In September, a trainer from your team must present a recommendation to the Personnel Director as to which external consultant you propose to develop and deliver a new course to meet some sales training needs. Assume that Brian, the trainer to whom you will delegate this task, understands sales training but he and the others are too busy to handle it within the time required. You have already identified a short list of three consultants for consideration and all of them are known to Brian. Let's say that Brian has low experience in decision making (knows the basic process), and has reasonable experience in making presentations (four previous presentations to senior managers). What checkpoints would you set?

_____

_____

_____

Our suggested checkpoints would be:

(a) **Approve the criteria for the decision** After Brian has developed the criteria, but before the detailed analysis of pros and cons of each consultant.

(b) **Review recommendation and approve** After Brian has arrived at a recommendation, but before preparing the presentation.

(c) **Review the content of the presentation** After the presentation is prepared, but before delivery. If required by Brian, a dummy run before September.

(d) **Review the outcome** On return from the conference, to discuss the meeting and outcome. This is not strictly a 'problem prevention' type of checkpoint because it is after the event, but it is important nevertheless. It may well indicate ways of preventing any problems in future presentations.

Please remember that the checkpoints set should generally operate **before the event**, not after. They are there to **prevent** potential difficulties, not 'shut the door after the horse has bolted'.

On one of our courses this year, a syndicate group had to make a very complex decision in an exercise and then present it to the 'Directors' of the mythical company for whom they were working. The group craftily 'delegated' this presentation to one of their members, we will call her Pam (who was unfortunate enough to leave the room just before that stage!). The group intended to ask her to handle the presentation, and just let her prepare whilst they did something else. When Pam returned, the group gave her the bad news, which she took very well. She then said two things that really had a major influence on the presentation. *'Okay, but I'm not going to the loo ever again. I need two things from you. I need a dummy run with you acting as the 'Directors' and you must ensure that you give me tough questions, just as they would. Secondly, we have only been given 15 minutes to make our case, so I need time control signals, especially in the last five minutes. If we run out of time our recommendation stands NO chance. Will you do what I need?'* The group were extremely impressed, agreed to everything (wouldn't you?), and duly did as they were asked.

The presentation that Pam made was excellent; clear, persuasive, and finished with two minutes to spare. She effectively handled a couple of very tough questions from us which even her group had not anticipated. We think that this was largely due to the confidence that Pam had gained from the difficult dummy run session with the group.

This story illustrates the use of effective checkpoints in delegation. In order to successfully complete the 'delegated' task, Pam decided that she needed two checkpoints, one before and, broadly, one during the actual presentation. Pam had identified three potential areas of difficulty; the unfamiliarity of the situation, the difficult questions she was likely to get, and the need to get the point across within 15 minutes. She knew that a dummy run would reduce the unfamiliarity, give her practise with tough questions, and verify that the ideas could be put over within 15 minutes. These actions reduce the likelihood of a problem arising but, just in case she spoke too much or was side-tracked by questions, the time signals from the group would have alerted her to that situation.

We knew, as did her group, that it was the first 'senior management' presentation that Pam had ever made. The other group complimented Pam and her group afterwards for 'choosing the professional' in their team!

Pam was justifiably delighted with the outcome which was due to effective checkpoints set by her and the support she received from her group.

ALLOW AMPLE TIME FOR THE DISCUSSION

Sounds obvious, but people often don't do it. Partly, this is due to the other pressures on our time; partly it can be due to a bit of optimism.

Other pressures on our time

Most people would agree that there never seems to be enough time but delegation is important, and it takes time *to do it properly*. We have never known an effective delegation discussion take less than 15 minutes but some people seem to try and do it in five minutes. All we can really say is that rushed delegation is likely to cause far more problems for the manager and the delegatee so the old adage applies: 'If it's worth doing, it's worth doing well'.

Optimism

This is the 'He won't have any problem with this one' approach. He might not, but what if he does have concerns about his ability to do it. Often, our time estimates are about right but there is little margin for safety. Delegation is often just as much about handling people's feelings as it is about discussing the actual task, and dealing properly with feelings can take time.

Suppose you allow the barest minimum time, and it transpires that one of your team unexpectedly has real doubts about their ability to handle the job. Would you really want to say, 'Look, Bill. I'll have to pick this up with you later. I haven't got time at the moment as I've got to get to a meeting' unless you really had to?

When preparing for the discussion, there is a guideline that may well prove useful:

> **Decide how much time you think the delegation discussion will need, then ... *double it!***

If you use this guideline and the discussion actually takes less time, you have gained.

HELPING AND ENCOURAGING THEM TO PREPARE FOR THE MAIN DISCUSSION

Most managers appreciate that, in order to delegate effectively, they have to prepare. Sometimes however they forget that they should give the delegatee the chance to prepare as well (where necessary), and encourage them to do so.

There are some situations where preparation by the delegatee is not really feasible, or needed. Some tasks are simply too urgent to permit much advanced warning to the person to whom you intend to delegate. Even here there is something to watch and maybe question. The manager might have known about the deadline for two weeks but by the time he or she is ready to start on the task, only one day is left. If they had thought about who would be involved earlier, there would have been ample time for that person to do some preparation. In addition, the delegatee may not need much (or even any) preparation time because either

- they are fully experienced in that task (level 4), having done it successfully on numerous previous occasions, or
- they are going to do the job entirely with you (level 1) because they have never done anything like it before, so there is little they would be able to do beforehand.

When is preparation by the delegatee needed, and why?

Broadly, when prior work by them will help to meet the objective that you have in mind. Typically there are two situations where prior work by the delegatee should help:

- where they have some experience and their involvement is necessary to gain the commitment that you need, and
- where your primary objective is to help one of your team to develop skills/knowledge.

Let's start with 'involvement'. There seems to be a strong link between involvement and commitment. The more we involve someone in a process, the more they are likely to be committed to the plan and outcome because they feel a personal responsibility. This involvement can start at the preparation stage by asking the person concerned to think about how he or she would tackle the task, what resources would be needed, etc. The plan is then theirs, not yours.

Now for 'development'. A colleague and friend of many years standing had one of those sayings that just seem to stick in your mind:

> **'As a trainer, I'm no expert, so I can teach people nothing. All I can do is provide the opportunity for them to *learn*.'**

'Development', to us, is providing that 'opportunity to learn'. The person may not have very much experience but that does not mean they cannot work out roughly what might be required to complete the task successfully. I have never driven a double-decker bus but I can make a reasonable guess at what I would need to do or learn in order to drive one. A bus driver would certainly be able to tighten up my plan. Which is better **learning**; let me work out most of it for myself then help me, or just tell me how to do it? Some people only seem to rely on the 'tell' method.

107

It is important to remember that, in order to prepare, the person must be able to answer, or find the answers to, the questions that you might ask them to consider.

What should the delegatee prepare?

Much depends on the task, the person, and your objective but what follows is a checklist of possible questions that you might include in your initial briefing discussion for them to consider.

CHECKLIST OF POSSIBLE QUESTIONS TO HELP THE DELEGATEE TO PREPARE:

- What would you see as the objective (result) here?
- How would you go about achieving it (the plan)?
- What are your present skills / knowledge in this area?
- Are there any skills / knowledge gaps with which you might need help? If so, what are they?

- What help do you need from me, or others?
- What extra resources are needed,if any?
- What authority do you need from me?
- What potential dificulties do you anticipate, and what can be done to prevent/minimise them?
- At what stages in your plan do we need to meet?
- What do you think that you will gain from doing this task?
- How do you feel about doing this task?

As no checklist will suit every situation, make a note below of any additional or alternative questions that you want to include:

_____

_____

_____

_____

_____

_____

What help and encouragement should you provide?

Everyone needs a bit of encouragement now and then. This is particularly true of delegation. Even very experienced people have that tiny nagging doubt that something might go wrong this time. We have said this before but it's worth repeating; if you don't sound as if you believe that they can handle it, why should they believe it?

Encouragement is important throughout the entire task, not just during the preparation stage. However, it is particularly important here as it starts the whole process off on a positive note.

So what help should you provide, during their preparation for the main discussion? This depends on your objective, the deadline, and their level of experience/ability. It may also depend on the amount of help that they ask for, if they are operating at level 3.

An example might help to illustrate the help you might provide at different levels of experience/ability. Let's take the need to prepare your monthly Departmental Report, within five working days from now. Assume that you have four people who report to you who are all at different levels of experience/ability.

Linda deputises in your absence, has effectively compiled the entire report on your behalf many times before, and is completely 'comfortable' in doing so. However since Linda last did the report for you, you have added a section on long-term plans that she has not seen.

Linda is already at level 4 so is unlikely to need to do any preparation before you brief her for this month's report. Consequently, no need for her to prepare means no need of help from you. You could go straight into the main discussion, i.e. quick review then concentrating primarily on the new section.

John is an experienced team member and provides you with a monthly report on the activities in his section that you do not need to alter. He has produced the report in draft form once for you but missed out one of the sections completely, which you corrected in time. He has since produced the final report once but seemed to concentrate rather too much on what his own section was achieving, and saying little about the other sections.

John is at level 3 so would benefit from some preparation prior to tackling the task. As he has reasonable prior experience of the task, he should be able to deal with the 'preparation' questions unaided, but should be encouraged to ask for help if required. It would be interesting to see if/what he has learned from the two previous 'mistakes'.

109

Chantelle has compiled the actual figures for the main section of the report before but gave them to you for inclusion. She has a good understanding of the company report procedure, and has compiled one or two progress reports for customers.

Chantelle is at level 2 (knows the basics) but has quite a long way to go before she is at level 3. She will probably need quite a bit of help from you in order to answer the 'preparation' questions, in order to link her present experience with the requirements of a departmental report.

Ivan has no experience of writing reports nor of the company procedure concerning the format for departmental reports. However he produces clear, well-structured letters, and is keen to learn new things.

Ivan is at level 1; no experience of departmental reports but has the will to learn. Expecting any preparation before the main discussion would probably be rather unfair; he might not even be able to *start* answering the questions. You would probably go straight into the main discussion, explaining the company procedure, format, content, etc. as you go.

The discussion itself: analysis of a delegation discussion

We have so far looked only at preparation for the discussion. Now we will get on to what many people see as the key issue of **handling the actual discussion**. You have probably encountered a delegation discussion before, either as the manager or as the person on the receiving end. Before we look at how an effective discussion should go, you might like to assess your existing knowledge in this area.

What follows is a description of a situation and a transcript of a (fictional) delegation discussion. Read through it and, in the space provided afterwards, note down what you believe to be wrong with it.

THE SITUATION

Paul is the Sales Manager of a firm of clothing manufacturers, and has a team of ten sales people reporting to him. This morning he has received an enquiry from a large, national chain of department stores for the supply of children's clothing to all of their stores. If the order is won, it would put the chain amongst the top six customers. Normally Paul would personally handle an enquiry of this size, but Paul has a problem. Today is Tuesday and tomorrow he is going abroad with the Sales Director on business for two weeks. The buyer for the chain of stores, Pat Rhodes, is out of the office until Tuesday of next week and wants to discuss the quotation next Wednesday, so that the order can be placed by the end of next week with the selected supplier. They have stated in the enquiry that they are looking for quality clothing, with modern designs at a reasonable price, and a consistent supply throughout the year. Paul is confident that the firm can win this order, and intends to delegate it to Andrea.

Andrea is the senior salesperson in Paul's team and would have the responsibility for managing the account if the quotation is successful. She has five years' sales experience and has handled enquiries before, but not those involving this level of money as they are normally handled by Paul.

THE DELEGATION DISCUSSION BETWEEN PAUL (SALES MANAGER) AND ANDREA (SENIOR SALESPERSON)

Paul: *'Ah. good. Come in, Andrea. Sit yourself down. Have I got a challenge for you!'*

Andrea: *'Morning, Paul. I've just come back from XYZ Limited and have managed to get a repeat order for those 15,000 shirts . . .'*

P *'Sorry. Haven't got time for that now. I need to explain what I want you to do so I can go down and pick up the tickets for my trip to the USA. Good, eh.*

'Now, you know the chain store Blinks and Blonks? Well, they have just given us an enquiry for £35,000 of children's clothes per month, and I have chosen you to handle the enquiry and the meeting with their buyer, Pat Rhodes. It will be really good for your development. What do you think about that then?'

A Stunned silence. *'Well, umm, er, that's a large order but I'm not sure I can handle that. I've never . . .'*

P *'Of course you can handle it. It's vital that we get that order so I'll explain exactly what you need to do.'*

A *'But Paul, I've never handled an enquiry this big and, as for the meeting . . .'*

P *'Look. How many more times – you can cope, for goodness sake. Stop whinging. Besides there's no one else left who can do it anyway so it's down to you. The Sales Director and I will both be in the USA. Now let's get on with it, shall we? You need to put the quote together by tonight, show it to me, then go and see their buyer next Wednesday!'*

A *'What about the meeting I have planned with XYZ for next Wednesday, Paul. They are customers too you know. You can't just mess people about like that. I can't just . . .'*

P *'Andrea, you are starting to make me angry. This is big business we are talking here not the little order we get from XYZ. You have got to get your priorities straight, girl.'*

A *'The XYZ order I have just brought back with me is worth £75,000 and there's more to come. Call that little do you, Paul?'*

P *'So, Andrea, you have just proved to me that you CAN cope with large orders so you'll be all right then, won't you? You will just have to move that meeting with XYZ. With your obvious selling skills that won't be a problem.'*

'Now let's talk about the quotation. I have mapped one out for you based on their enquiry, so you talk to the production people about deliveries and costs, then fill in the figures. You do understand, don't you?'

A *'I suppose so but what about . . .'*

P *'Now, the meeting with the buyer. Make a big point of our quality and the fact that we guarantee deliveries. Make sure you cover the other big names that we supply. Oh, yes, and check you have got an order form with you. Whatever you do, get him to sign the order before you leave his office. Smile sweetly at him!'*

A *'But what if SHE wants to talk about discounts; Pat is a woman, you know. I don't know how far I can go at that level.'*

P *'Oh, excuse me! If SHE is not happy with the price we quote, you had better ring me in the USA if you can find me through the hotel there. The Sales Director's secretary probably has some sort of itinerary.'*

A *'Isn't Pat expecting YOU at this meeting, Paul? After all she did write to you.'*

P *'Look, just phone her on Tuesday and explain I'm away. I can't do it, can I? So get that quote ready for me by tonight and I'll approve it before I leave.'*

A *'Thank you, Paul!'*

What was wrong with the preceding delegation discussion between Paul and Andrea?

_____

_____

_____

_____

_____

_____

_____

_____

_____

_____

112

_____

_____

_____

_____

_____

_____

_____

_____

_____

_____

_____

_____

_____

_____

_____

Our view as to what is wrong with Paul's approach in the discussion

Just about everything really! (In fairness, Paul did set a measurable objective – get him to sign the order.)

Paul's overall style Very much the 'tell' approach, with little credit to Andrea for her existing skills and knowledge, which probably put her at level 3. There could, and should have been far more involvement. His questions are very directive; loaded towards getting the answers that he wants. Paul went further than straightforward 'tell', demeaning her and being sarcastic; there was no justification at all.

Introduction The opening should have helped put Andrea at ease before 'dropping the bombshell'. Opening with 'Have I got a challenge for you!' is likely to worry the bravest of us. This sort of 'pressure' could make Andrea feel it is an impossibility rather than a 'challenge'. Indeed, Paul applied pressure throughout the discussion, i.e. 'It's vital. It must be done now. I haven't got time. You must do it, etc.' Paul was not interested in HER bit of good news regarding the XYZ order and didn't even really listen to her. Had he done so the atmosphere could have been entirely different, and he could have used this success to the best advantage, i.e. motivation, justifiable praise, confidence booster, and proof of ability.

113

Background Paul then went on to explain the background (the enquiry) and what he wanted Andrea to do. Saying 'it will be good for your development' didn't help. There was no explanation as to *why* it would be good for Andrea's development. This job probably *would* be a good challenging, developmental activity if Angela was looking to progress within sales. As the conversation progressed, Andrea would have felt that the only reason she had been asked to do it was purely because of the absence of Paul and the Sales Director.

Main body Andrea expressed understandable concern about her ability to handle the task. Instead of actually handling the feelings, Paul simply said 'Of course you can handle it' as though that was the answer to everything. Paul also seemed to think that telling Andrea how to do it would be the answer. She might already *know* how to do it but is unsure about her ability to cope well. He didn't try to explain WHY he thought she could cope. She still wasn't comfortable so Paul accused her of 'whinging'; a great help!

He then said 'anyway there's no one else left', so now we have got to his *real* reason, as far as Andrea is concerned. At this point Paul goes back into telling her what to do; he doesn't think to ask for her views.

Andrea now moves on to a clash in priorities (the meeting with XYZ on Wednesday) which was a completely valid concern. Paul sarcastically tries to brush this concern aside, and when Andrea shows why XYZ is just as important, Paul throws it back in her face rather than compliment her for doing a good job. The clash in priorities was not satisfactorily resolved, in Andrea's eyes.

Paul has 'mapped out the quotation' (maybe trying to help in a weird sort of way) but by treating her like an idiot, would only reinforce her lack of confidence. No respect at all for her existing experience or ability. With regard to the meeting, Andrea has experience with her 'smaller' customers so broadly knows how to handle it. Her concern is not how to sell, but with her own confidence to operate at this level (large sums of money involved, large order discounts, etc.). Instead of giving her the authority (with limits) that she needs to make decisions in the meeting, Paul says 'phone me if you can find me'. If you were Andrea and Pat raises the issue of discounts, how would you feel knowing that you might not even be able to locate him and possibly lose the order as a result? Andrea is an experienced salesperson and simply needed some guidelines and limits of authority from Paul, e.g. 'If the issue of discounts arises we would normally go up to 15 per cent for a 12-month order. Do the best deal you can within that. If Pat demands more and you are stuck, I have spoken to our Managing Director and you can ring him. That will save you trying to chase me all over America. Is that OK with you?'

Andrea obviously knows more about Pat Rhodes (and probably Blinks and Blonks) than Paul appreciates; hence the comment '*Pat* is a woman'. Paul is sarcastic again rather than probe to find out how much Andrea knows. Incidentally, this could have all come out right at the start. Do you remember Paul's early rhetorical question 'you know the chain store Blinks and Blonks?' If he had paused for breath, he might just have found out how much Andrea already knows.

When Andrea raises the issue of Pat expecting Paul, not Andrea, to attend the meeting, Paul again tells her what to do rather than asking for her thoughts. Andrea might have preferred Paul to write a brief letter of explanation to Pat.

Closing Yet another smack in the mouth with a wet cod for poor old Andrea. A wonderful note on which to end. Well done, Paul!

Conclusion Andrea would probably have tried to do the best job she could (in spite of Paul's approach) but would certainly have felt that the job had been 'dumped' on her. Sad, when she could have viewed it very differently. The main concern is that of the 'discount' situation. If it arises (and it probably would), Andrea could lose the order because of the difficulties; and she knows it! When Paul returns from the USA, he might well be in for a double shock. The B & B order might have gone elsewhere . . . and so might Andrea.

Overview of the delegation discussaion

We are all different and would all handle a delegation discussion in a different way. That is as it should be. Your own personality/style of management, the task requirements, the person to whom you are delegating, and whether there was any preparation by the delegatee all play a part in the approach used, so to try and identify the right approach would be impossible. There is no such thing! We will try to outline some of the implications of these variables below.

YOUR OWN PERSONALITY/STYLE OF MANAGEMENT

If you are a fairly forceful character by nature, you will probably be used to clearly explaining the objective and task. You may also be very good at setting up controls. These are vital at level 1 but you may need to modify your natural approach when delegating at the other levels where questions rather than instructions are important. This 'switch' is particularly important where, in the preparation stage, you decide that their involvement is important for commitment, because involvement equals questions.

On the other hand, you may be a very democratic sort of person who likes to involve people. You may well ask very good questions naturally but remember that if the person is inexperienced, they may not know enough to be able to answer them. In this case you will have to be rather more directive than you would normally be. You may also like to let people set their own controls. Again, the person may not know how to do that if the situation is unfamiliar, so you might need to suggest how to do it.

THE TASK REQUIREMENTS AND THE PERSON

If the task is familiar and the person is at level 4, then only a very brief discussion is necessary; you don't need to spend time building confidence when it is already there. If the task is unfamiliar and the person has no experience (level 1), the discussion will be fairly instruction-oriented, and lengthy; the person needs to understand how to do it. If the task will represent a challenge for the person who unjustly lacks confidence in themselves, the discussion will major on handling their feelings; it takes time and factual evidence of ability to build confidence.

PREPARATION BY THE DELEGATEE

If the person to whom you intend to delegate has been given the chance to do some preparation before you both meet, and they have done a good job, you will probably spend much of the meeting hearing their views and building on their ideas. Much of the groundwork has been done in your original briefing to them. If there was no need or opportunity for prior preparation by them, you may well feel that you need to use most, if not all, of the guidelines that follow.

These variables quite rightly affect our approach. However there are some useful guidelines that help to make the discussion as effective as it can be. These guidelines are not laws written on tablets of stone. If every manager followed them exactly every time there would be a danger of producing 'delegation clones', and the manager would not be responding to the variables that we have already discussed.

We will discuss each of the guidelines in detail in the following sections. At the end of the chapter there will be the two summaries covering the key points to remember

- during preparation, and
- during the discussion.

Please remember these guidelines will not all apply equally to every situation; we cannot stress this enough. Please see them as areas for consideration. Only you can decide when, and to what extent, each applies.

Starting the discussion off on the right foot

The opening is critical. It sets the atmosphere for the rest of the discussion. The aim here is to put the person at ease, and outline the purpose of the discussion.

PUTTING THE PERSON AT EASE

Putting someone at ease is really helping them to arrive fairly quickly at a point where they are really listening to you, and not worrying about some other issue on their mind.

Have you ever driven through the same old set of traffic lights on your way to work and, as soon as you passed them, gulped and wondered if they were at red? You were probably thinking of something else so were not really concentrating on your driving. That's what we mean! (For what it's worth, you may well have sub-consciously registered the fact the lights were at green, but we wouldn't recommend that you rely on it, and our 'friends in blue' certainly wouldn't either!)

Your approach to this opening phase of helping someone to settle down is likely to depend on whether or not they had any prior warning of the discussion, i.e. you asked them to do some preparation. If you have previously asked someone to do some preparation prior to this delegation discussion, they know the purpose of the meeting when they arrive at your office, but might still be somewhat nervous about handling the task. They will probably need some time to settle. Asking them how their preparation went lets them discuss any issues they might have. You do not necessarily have to resolve their issues there and then though. If you know that the issue will be better handled at a later stage in your discussion, explain that, and why, and check that they are happy for you to delay discussing it. As long as the issue will be covered at some stage in your conversation, people are usually happy to accept the fact. Throughout the discussion, you should be able to link to their preparation.

The need to put someone at ease is even more important if there was no prior warning, i.e. an urgent task has just arisen and you need to talk to the person to whom you will delegate it straight away. So, out you go to his or her desk and say something like 'Ken, can you pop into my office for a minute please?'

You may now encounter the dreaded 'Boss's Office Syndrome'.

What is Ken's immediate thought likely to be? Usually something like 'What's up? Have I done anything wrong?' As Ken walks to your office with the others looking on, he might just convince himself that he is about to meet the 'hanging judge'. You don't want a lengthy discussion at his desk, but you can remove the basic concern once in your office. 'Ken, I need your help on a new job that has just come up. Before I cover that, how are things out there?' . . . But you might be thinking, *why ask how are things? Won't that side-track the conversation?* Only briefly probably, but it is important. The person to whom you intend to delegate may perhaps not see you very often so they may well have some news, or some issue that they want to talk about. A brief discussion will cost you very little extra time but it is important to them, and will help to put them at ease for the main discussion. If you know that the issue they have raised will be covered within your plan for the discussion, explain that it will be covered later, and why, and check that they are happy with that.

117

But what if some other entirely separate *major* issue arises right at the beginning of the discussion?

It can happen. The only thing that you can do is to decide on the relative priority (in terms of importance and urgency) of the two issues, the task to be delegated versus the issue that they have raised. You may have allowed enough time for the discussion to enable you to deal with both the discussion and the issue they have raised. However, life is not always so kind. It may be necessary to temporarily 'shelve' the delegation discussion , to choose someone else to carry out the delegated task, or to get someone else to handle the issue that has been raised.

Let's assume that the person has now settled down and you are ready to continue. The second phase of the opening is to explain/review the background and purpose of the discussion

EXPLAIN/REVIEW THE BACKGROUND AND PURPOSE OF THE DISCUSSION

If you have asked someone to prepare for this meeting, you have already covered this in your initial meeting with them. You may just need to remind them of the key points via a quick review. If, however, this is the first meeting, you will need to cover four areas under 'Background and Purpose':

- explain the background
- why the task is being delegated
- why you have chosen them to do it, and
- the purpose of this discussion.

You already have the information you need to cover these points from your own preparation.

Explain the background

Cover what the task is, how the job arose, with a brief outline of what is involved, and why it is important. It is important that you show some enthusiasm for the task. If you don't believe that it is worth doing, why should they? There are different forms of 'enthusiasm'. Some people appear to equate enthusiasm with some sort of all-singing, all-dancing act. If you are naturally an extrovert, bubbly sort of character, terrific; just be yourself. On the other hand, you might be a quieter, more reserved type of person. Feigning over-the-top enthusiasm will be spotted, and treated accordingly. You can still show just as much enthusiasm by explaining why you personally believe the task to be important.

Why the task is being delegated

Explain the reason why it is being delegated, i.e. for development, because you need help, because you are unable to do it personally this time, etc. Please remember to be honest! If it is a boring, mundane job on which you simply need help to get it out on time, our belief is, say so! There is nothing worse than being told 'It will be good for your development', when it obviously will NOT help it at all, and so is seen as 'dressing it up'.

Why you have chosen them to do it

If you don't explain this, they will pit there own interpretation on the reason, which may well be wrong. If appropriate, it might also be useful at this point to discuss what benefit there is for them in doing the task, e.g. they want to improve their presentation skills and this task will provide the opportunity to do so.

The purpose of this discussion

119

This is really what you want to achieve *from this meeting;* the objective for the task itself will come in later. It usually goes something like . . . 'So the purpose of our discussion today is to produce a plan together for the presentation on 15 June and make sure that you are happy about carrying it out, with help from me if you need it.'

Before moving on to the main body of the discussion, it is worth briefly summarising the key points so far to ensure that everything is clear to the delegatee, and identify any issues that might have been generated which will need to be resolved.

The main body of the discussion

The following guidelines are not in any particular order; they are all important in different situations. To help you, we have outlined a broad structure for the discussion later in this chapter.

ENSURE THAT THE TASK IS FEASIBLE

Ask the delegatee about their workload and the implications of it with regard to the task you are delegating. If they have a vital meeting on the key day, there is little point continuing with the discussion (unless someone else can handle it for them). You might think that this should have shown up during preparation. Maybe, but arrangements change. Check!

If the task is fairly complicated, you may well have to jointly produce the plan and agree how much time will be needed before you can discuss the effect on their present workload/deadlines and decide feasibility.

If the task is feasible but their work will have to be reorganised to accommodate the delegated task, ask for their ideas as to how best this can be handled. Beware of taking on this work personally though. You might end up with more work than you are delegating. That does not mean that you should do nothing to help but ask yourself whether your involvement is really justified before you say 'Yes'. Ask them to consider whether there is anyone else in the team who could help them. An example of where your involvement might be fully justified could be where someone wants to 'dummy-run' a presentation with some feedback before the main event. You might be the only person with the right experience, or they ask you because they trust your judgement.

REVIEW THEIR SKILLS AND KNOWLEDGE

At the preparation stage, you will have considered what the task needs and what skills and knowledge the person already has. Any gaps should already have been identified. Ask for their views, and, to start positive, ask them to outline their strengths first. Then ask them what the task needs (if they can answer that), and finally whether they foresee any gaps or weaknesses.

Try to ensure that they give themselves credit for their strengths and know how they apply to this particular task. Ask them what can be done to help any gaps or weaknesses that they identify. They may need some coaching from you either now or during the task; 'now' if it is necessary to get them started, 'during' if you are using the building block approach discussed in an earlier chapter, to help them learn in stages.

If there are any key strengths or weaknesses that they have not identified, you may well need to raise them if they could affect the overall result. Where possible, try to give actual examples to illustrate your point.

MAKING THEIR RESPONSIBILITIES CLEAR

When briefing them to prepare, or in the opening of this discussion, you broadly outlined the task. At some point their specific responsibilities will need to be discussed and agreed. It is at this point that you will probably agree their objective (clear, measurable and realistic, with a deadline and constraints if any) for the task.

SHOW CONFIDENCE IN THEM

This is important throughout the whole discussion. The difficulty is that most people know that a manager should do this but some people seem to have a knack of making it sound insincere; 'Fred, you're a good chap. I know you'll do a grand job on this.' If *you* don't appear to believe that they can do the task, then why should *they* believe it either. It is very easy to say 'show confidence' but how do you do it *genuinely?*

As we have said before, there is a big difference between praise and flattery. The example above is flattery. To show genuine confidence in someone's ability to do the task, you have got to prove why you believe that they can cope. They may never have done this particular task before but you have decided already that they have the ability. Ask yourself 'why do I think they can cope?', then use it!

As an example, suppose you are asking one of your team to deputise for you during a two week absence from the office and they are unsure if they can handle it. Let's say they have acted as 'stand-in' for you for three days in the past and made a good job of it. You can link to this occasion, talk about the issues they had to handle, praise them for what they did well, and then help them see that the issues that they had to handle over that three-day period are unlikely to be very different to those that might arise over this two-week period.

121

GOOD QUESTIONS ARE VITAL

This is true, even at level 1, where you are taking the person through a totally unfamiliar task. Although you may not ask as many questions for involvement as you would with people who have a higher level of experience, you still need to make sure that they really understand what you are teaching them. Secondly, *no experience* does not necessarily mean *no ability*.

Note below what you think are the **main types of question** that would be useful when delegating, and the **purpose** of each.

Type	Purpose
_____	_____
_____	_____
_____	_____
_____	_____
_____	_____

Types of questions useful in delegation, their definition, examples, and their purpose

There are quite a few different types of question. What we have tried to do here is identify those which are particularly useful when trying to delegate. They are:

■ Open
■ Probing
■ Clarifying
■ Closed

Note: some *additional* types of question will be covered in Chapter 11 'Handling Difficulties' as they are particularly appropriate to this situation.

Open

(a) Definition Questions that usually collect *general* information. They usually start with 'what', 'where', 'when', 'who', 'how', or 'why'. Another useful opening is, 'can you tell me about . . .', as it lets them put things in their own words.

(b) Examples: 'How do you feel about handling this, Janet?', or 'Can you tell me about the last time you produced a sales proposal?'

(c) Purpose: Open questions are the equivalent of throwing out a fishing net into the surf, but you don't know which. or how many, 'fish' you will catch. Open questions explore the general area and 'net' information for you, but you may well have to follow up with a 'probing' question in order to get to the specifics that you need.

Probing

(a) Definition: Questions that collect *specific* information.

(b) Examples: 'What exactly do you see as the objective?', 'What will you do if David arrives late for the meeting as usual?', or 'Why do you feel that you won't cope with this presentation?'

(c) Purpose: These home in on a specific 'fish'. They provide you with concrete information on facts and opinions, and are used to uncover key issues.

Clarifying

(a) Definition These ensure that what is said is actually understood.

(b) Examples 'So, Tim, you will take that meeting on the 15th, will you?', or 'You seem to feel that you might have difficulty with the format, but not the content. Is that right?'

(c) Purpose We all know that what might be said is not necessarily understood as we intend. Have you ever asked someone to do something for you, but found that the outcome was entirely different? *That* is why clarification is so important! There is a problem attached to this sort of question though. Many people tend not to use this sort of question very much as they are afraid that they will appear 'dim'. Providing that it is not over-done, people appear to see it as 'showing interest'.

It is important to clarify when:

■ you are not sure that you fully understand what they are saying, or feeling
■ you are not sure if they understand you
■ you are about to disagree with their idea. Clarifying before the disagreement can be useful because you may find that you had misinterpreted and there is nothing about which you actually disagree.

Closed

123

A word of warning. This last type of question has its place but *should not be over-done!*

(a) Definition: These confirm or deny something and usually result in 'Yes' or 'No' responses.

(b) Examples: 'Can you finish that by Friday?', or 'Are you familiar with the company procedure for monthly reports?'

(c) Purpose: Ideal for checking some straightforward issue, where a simple 'yes' or 'no' will suffice. Unfortunately, for some managers, these can form the largest proportion of the questions asked in the discussion. Consequently, very little is learned about how the delegatee really thinks or feels. Suppose, for example, you say something like, 'Can you handle this for me?' Are they really going to say anything other than 'yes'? They might but it is fairly unlikely. Please try to avoid using closed questions when you are trying to check how the person might feel.

THE IMPORTANCE OF SUMMARIES

In the last section, we covered clarifying questions and their importance in the discussion. Summaries perform a similar role and, in a sense, are rather like a grand form of 'clarifying'. The clarifying question checks understanding on one factor, whereas a summary generally checks understanding on several. For example:

Clarify 'Did you say that you will finish your draft report by *Friday*?'

Summary 'Let's just summarise. We have agreed that you will finish the draft report by Friday; we will meet and discuss it at 10am on Monday 15th; and you will then produce the final version by the following Wednesday. Have I got that right?'

So *when* should you summarise then?

Basically, whenever it helps both of you; NOT just at the end. A summary is usually helpful at the end of each 'section' of the discussion, to ensure everything is clear before moving on. If there is any misunderstanding it is better to identify and deal with it before leaving a section than to discover it much later and have to backtrack.

INVOLVE THEM IN THE DISCUSSION TO WHATEVER EXTENT IS FEASIBLE

Involvement depends, to a large extent, on how much someone already knows (or can imagine) about the task. The more a person knows about the task you are delegating , the more should they be able to 'dictate their own destiny'. However, that does not mean that there can be no involvement just because someone has no experience. They may be able to 'imagine' what is involved. So involve them to whatever extent is possible in preparing the plan.

Involvement at level 1

Someone who has virtually no experience of the task at all might well be able to propose the BROAD steps required on which you can build. In this way, the plan is theirs rather than yours, even though they are going to do most of the task with you. Due to their lack of experience, they will need you to explain how the task is done before embarking on it with you. Any potential difficulties that they might face with any detailed work that they do for you are probably best discussed when you brief them for that particular aspect of the task. As an example, suppose that you are going to ask them to collect and enter data into a spreadsheet for you. When briefing them, you may need to explain where the data comes from and maybe some new spreadsheet commands they will not have used. Going through all of these points right at the start could be far more confusing than at the time (remember 'bite-sized chunks'?)

Involvement at level 2

They already know the basics, so should be able to make a significant contribution to the plan. They may also be able to suggest some of the major checkpoints but may not yet know enough to cover all of the important ones. At this level they should be able to suggest some of the potential difficulties and actions to help. They may need help/guidance from you on how to actually carry out some of the less familiar aspects of the job. At this level of experience/ability, there is a fairly high likelihood of minor mistakes (major mistakes should be prevented by your guidance, and the controls you set). However, if they propose something that you know will result in a minor mistake, decide whether to try and prevent it, or to let them make it and learn from it.

At this level, and possibly at level 3, there is a trap for the manager into which it is very easy to fall. Their approach to the task may well be different from the way you would do it, so there is a strong temptation to say something like 'If I were you, I would do it like this...' Try and ask yourself whether their way will work, without causing a major problem. If so then, to gain commitment, let them do it their way, even though it may not be quite as efficient at first as your way.

Some years ago, a neighbour needed to move a garden shed from one side of the garden to the other. His plan was to 'bribe' five or six of us with vast quantities of beer to pick it up and carry it; it wasn't a big shed. Anyway the neighbour had a ten-year-old son who had never moved a shed in his life but saw some old rustic poles in the corner of the garden. He innocently said to his dad 'Why don't you lift the end of the shed, then I'll put a pole under it? We can roll it forward a bit, then I'll put another pole under and we can keep on rolling it to where you want it to be.' I'll never forgive him for doing me out of that beer! Just shows you though . . .

125

Involvement at level 3

The person has a reasonable level of experience and ability now. Most of the input to the planning phase can come from them. They will propose the steps, the controls, and decide what help they need from you. Their requests for help are likely to relate to the 'advanced' aspects of the task with which they are less familiar. Encourage them to identify any potential difficulties and suggest ways of handling those difficulties. Again, they might ask for help with this to ensure that they have not missed anything significant.

The principle at level 3 is to 'let them call the shots' and remember to watch out for the 'If I were you' trap! Correct their plan *only if it contains a major flaw.*

Involvement at level 4

They are fully experienced and 'comfortable' with their ability to handle the task. Detailed planning with you is not necessary, unless anything has changed since they last did the job. The discussion hinges on clarifying the objective (with any constraints) with them, a quick check on feasibility in the time available, confirm they still feel 'comfortable', fix a date for them to report back to you on the outcome, then 'let them go'!

JOINTLY PRODUCE A PLAN

This is one of the key parts of the delegation discussion for a variety of reasons which we will cover as we go. The objective should have been discussed/clarified already. If for some reason you haven't done so, please make sure that this IS done before you try to put the plan together.

Why is a plan needed?

An effective plan is important to ensure that the objective will be met on time and to the right standard. It also forms the basis for the controls, by identifying the various stages and their expected completion times/dates. We see the plan as a sort of road map; the route to your destination.

What should the plan include?

Three elements should be covered in the plan: the key tasks necessary, who is responsible for each key task, and the deadline for completion of each key task.

Key tasks. These are the important tasks which must be done in order to meet the objective. Please note the we are not talking about every aspect of the job, just the important ones. So , for example, the key tasks necessary to prepare and give a presentation to a customer might be:

- clarify the objective (including any constraints)
- research the topic (content, audience, etc.)
- Prepare the presentation (including any visual aids) in draft form
- 'dummy-run' to own manager and team
- finalise the presentation (any changes after the dummy run)
- deliver the presentation to the customer
- review the outcome with own manager.

The person responsible for each key task. Usually this will be the delegatee, but the manager might justifiably take responsibility for a particular key task on which the person needs help.

The deadline for completion of each key task. This is the date by which each of the key tasks must be completed if the deadline for the overall objective is to be met.

The plan should show WHAT, WHO and BY WHEN

- *What* are the key tasks
- *Who* is responsible for each key task
- *By when* must each key task be completed.

DISCUSS POTENTIAL DIFFICULTIES

127

This is necessary in order to reduce the chances of the task going horribly wrong. The idea is to anticipate major potential difficulties and then work out actions which will prevent them arising (or reduce the likelihood), and to identify actions which will deal with them if, despite the attempts at prevention, they still arise.

As we mentioned in the earlier sections on 'involvement', you may need to identify them personally, or the person to whom you are delegating may be capable of doing so.

GIVE THEM ADEQUATE AUTHORITY

This is vital because responsibility without authority is unfair, and could even make an otherwise challenging task, an impossibility. Consider the steps of the plan that you have both prepared and decide where 'authority' is needed. Then decide what the limits of that authority might be and what form it should take. A phone call or a brief memo from you might help. For example, suppose that you are off on holiday for two weeks. A note to your team, with a copy to your manager, saying that Linda is standing-in for you and has the power to make management decisions in your name (or however you prefer to put it) might well make life easier for Linda. You trust her to deputise, so why not trust her with the power?

You might be forgiven for thinking that any decent manager would do some-thing like that. Some managers just don't; they don't want to, or they don't even think of it. To prove the point, an example. Some time ago, a friend was acting as deputy for his Sales Manager (one of three) who was on holiday. The Sales Director called a sales meeting which was attended by the deputy plus the other two managers. The objective was to achieve a 10 per cent increase in overall sales revenue by revising sales targets in each region. Due to the nature of the three sales regions, it would not be sensible to apply a blanket 10 per cent across all three regions. The region that was repre-sented by the deputy was justifiably asked to cover a larger increase; around 25 per cent. At this point, the deputy hesitated; not because he disagreed but because he had not been given the authority to make such decisions. He explained this to the meeting. They understood but needed his view which, of course, he did not want to quote in case he said the 'wrong thing', from the viewpoint of his own manager. The director could have mandated the increase but understood and reluctantly delayed the final decision until the manager returned from holiday, even though the targets needed to go up even more because of the delay.

Ask yourself how you would have felt as the deputy in that meeting; know-ing you should make a decision but lacking any authority to do so. Now, imagine that you are the Sales Director. What would you say to the Sales Manager when he gets back from his holiday?

DISCUSS AND AGREE THE CONTROLS

The title of this book is 'Letting Go, **Without Losing Control**', so this aspect of the discussion is vital. We have already referred to the need for effective controls in earlier chapters. This part of your dis-cussions identifies the necessary controls/checkpoints, and gains commitment to their use. The problem is that control operated by the manager can often be seen as 'interference'. Do you remember 'Long John Silver's parrot' in Chapter 4?

Rather than overload this chapter, we believe that the subject of 'control without interference' deserves its own chapter. If you feel that you need to understand more about 'controls' generally, and how to set them up, you might like to make a small deviation and read Chapter 10 'Control without Interference' before continuing with the rest of this chapter. If , however, you feel that you understand what a 'control' is, and how to set up controls effectively, then just carry on with this chapter.

Try to involve staff, if their experience permits, in the setting up of controls to ensure that the objective is achieved. If the person to whom you are delegating has experience of the task, they probably have the knowledge necessary to devise appropriate controls. In addition, they are likely to be more committed to a control system that *they* have devised, rather than to one devised by someone else. This avoids the need for frequent checks by the manager which can so often be seen as interference.

GIVE THEM A 'LIFELINE'

Whilst we do not want to interfere, neither should we abdicate. The controls cover the main checkpoints but what about the periods in between? People seem to feel more comfortable if they know that there is a 'lifeline' that they can use if they get into difficulties. Even the most experienced people sometimes like to discuss their thoughts with their manager, sometimes just for reassurance.

The most typical 'lifeline' goes something like, 'I know you can handle this but if you want to talk about anything, just come and see me. I will leave that up to you.' This puts the responsibility squarely on *them* to involve you when *they* believe it is necessary to do so, rather than to leave them sitting at their desk wondering whether they should or shouldn't ask for your opinion or help.

129

Ending the discussion effectively

All of the task planning issues should have been handled by now. There are, however, four very important areas left to cover. They are:

- summarise the key actions and agreements
- check how the person actually feels about doing the task
- arrange a follow-up meeting to take place after the event, and
- closing the discussion.

SUMMARISE KEY ACTIONS AND AGREEMENTS

You will have summarised at various stages throughout the discussion. This final summary covers the key actions, who is to act, and the key dates. It also picks up the agreements you have reached, i.e. limits of authority, how the controls will operate, when you decide to next meet, etc. This summary is important to close the 'task' side of the discussion and open the way for the next, rather less clear-cut, section.

CHECK HOW THE PERSON ACTUALLY FEELS ABOUT DOING THE TASK

It has to be said that some managers never seem to discuss **feelings;** they appear to believe that as long as the person knows how to do the task, that is enough. It doesn't always follow that just because we know HOW to do something, we necessarily WANT to do it, or feel comfortable about our ability to cope successfully. Imagine that someone explains everything involved in scuba diving to you, then leads you towards the swimming pool, where the gear is waiting on the side. How would you FEEL at this point?

Throughout the discussion, the manager should be gauging how the person feels about taking on the task, and responding to the comments (and 'vibes'). This final check before the discussion finishes is vital just in case you have missed the signals (or ignored them), and is very simple. 'Right, Peter, we have talked about what is involved in deputising for me next week. How do you actually *feel* about handling it now?'

A bit of nervousness is normal. The person will not feel really happy until they have completed the task successfully. Most of the time, all that is needed from you is a small amount of reassurance that you believe the person can cope, and cope well.

But what do you do if the worst happens? Suppose the person is still extremely unhappy about taking it on, despite the fact that you followed all of the previous guidelines. You really do have to ask whether you chose the right person for the task, in the first place. They lack commitment to the task, and/or belief in their own ability, despite everything you have said. The whole subject of motivation and gaining genuine commitment, within the context of delegation, is very important, and is dealt with in the next chapter, Chapter 9.

ARRANGE A FOLLOW-UP MEETING TO TAKE PLACE AFTER THE EVENT

It is always beneficial, in our opinion, for the manager and delegatee to meet after the event and review how things went, in order to reinforce strengths and discuss any areas for improvement. Suppose the person is going to give a presentation in your absence. The follow-up meeting after they have given the presentation will tell you what they have gained from the experience and help them to learn from it as well. Assuming it was successful, it also gives you a chance to say 'Thanks', something we believe to be important.

If you have not been involved in any of these follow-up meetings, Chapter 10 covers this type of discussion.

CLOSING THE DISCUSSION

This is simple but important. Remind them of the 'lifeline', and th. them for agreeing to help.

Below are the two summaries of the key points to remember

■ when preparing for the discussion, and

■ during the delegation discussion.

You might like to use these as checklists. Remember that not all of the factors will necessarily be applicable every time.

SUMMARY – CHAPTER 8

Preparing for the delegation discussion

■ Review the objective – clear, measurable (if possible), realistic, shows result, deadline and any constraints

■ Consider the background – task, person, any skill or knowledge gaps

■ Review the level:
  - level 1 – no experience
  - level 2 – knows the basics
  - level 3 – reasonable experience
  - level 4 – fully experienced

■ Decide the authority needed

■ Identify the control checkpoints (in case they miss any)

■ If feasible, encourage/help *them* to prepare

■ Allow ample time for the discussion

131

SUMMARY – CHAPTER 8

Guidelines for handling the delegation discussion

Starting the discussion off on the right foot:

■ Put the person at ease

■ If this is the first discussion, explain background: why task is needed, why that person, and purpose of discussion.

The main body of the discussion:

■ Check that the task is feasible, i.e. check workload issues

■ Review skills and knowledge, and any gaps

■ Make their responsibilities clear, or help them to clarify them

■ Show confidence in them – praise, not flattery

■ Ask effective questions, mainly open, probing, & clarifying

- Summarise whenever it helps both of you
- Involve them to whatever extent their experience allows, and decide whether to allow/prevent minor mistakes
- Jointly produce the plan, building on their ideas as much as possible
- Discuss potential difficulties, and decide how to handle
- Give them adequate authority
- Discuss and agree the controls
- Give them a 'lifeline'.

Ending the discussion effectively:

- Summarise the key actions and agreements
- Check how the person actually *feels* about doing the task
- Arrange a follow-up meeting to take place after the event
- Close; remind them of the 'lifeline', and thank them.

9

Getting genuine
commitment

Overview of this chapter

Deciding whether you have got *genuine* commitment from the person
to whom you are delegating is extremely hard. At some time or other,
all of us have probably said 'Yes' to something, just for a quiet life; not
necessarily because we actually *wanted* to do it. This chapter is about
helping the person arrive at a point where they genuinely *want* to do
the job, rather than feel that they **HAVE NO CHOICE BUT TO DO IT!**

Realistically, it is impossible to achieve this with every task for
every person to whom you might delegate. Occasionally you do have
to ask for help on boring, mundane jobs where you are unlikely to get
enthusiastic 'commitment'. This chapter is devoted to situations
where commitment *is* feasible.

What are the objectives for this chapter?

When you have read this chapter, you should:

- know how to identify and obtain genuine commitment
- know what motivates *you* and how to identify the key motivating
  factors for people in your team
- know what to do if you do not obtain genuine commitment.

What is covered in this chapter?

- What is *genuine* commitment?
- Identifying whether you need commitment or acceptance.

- How do you *obtain* this commitment?
- What if, despite your hard work, you don't actually *get* commitment?

What is *genuine* commitment?

One dictionary definition of 'commitment' is 'the act of pledging'. A pledge however can be willingly offered by the other party, or it can be 'extracted' by some means or other; foul or fair.

To illustrate the differences, without reference to delegation for a moment, consider charity donations. You are watching a telethon (a television event devoted to raising money for charities). You believe that what they are trying to do is worthwhile and you are quite enthusiastic to help, so you pick up the phone and donate some cash via your pet piece of plastic. You have shown genuine commitment; no one forced you, and you *wanted* to do it.

Alternatively, someone you know asks you, in front of other friends or colleagues, whether you will sponsor them on some event for a charity that you do not personally support (with much enthusiasm anyway). Is it fair to say that you are probably unlikely to say 'No'? You have made a commitment but, really, it has been 'extracted'. This sort of thing happens to everyone and we don't usually mind too much; the bit of pressure is light-hearted and taken as 'being in a good cause'. The question to ask is 'would you have donated the cash without that pressure, say, by post?' If the answer is 'not really', then the earlier commitment to sponsor was 'extracted'. You didn't partic-ularly want to do it, but felt that you *had* to do it.

The feelings generated in these two situations can be vastly differ-ent, and the same applies to delegation. In order to separate the two different 'levels' of commitment obtained in the two examples above, we have labelled them in a slightly different way, calling them '**gen-uine commitment**' (the telethon example) and '**acceptance**' (the sponsorship example).

WHAT IS THE DIFFERENCE BETWEEN GENUINE COMMITMENT AND ACCEPTANCE?

We see 'commitment' as a willing agreement by the delegatee to carry out the task to the best of their ability. 'Genuine' adds a further ele-ment; you have the impression that they really *want* to do it, and are enthusiastic about it. Another word for 'genuine' in this context, might be 'motivated'. One definition of 'motivation' that we use is 'encourag-ing someone to *willingly* and *enthusiastically* give the very best of which they are capable'. So once they reach this stage, we would say

134

that they are 'motivated'. You might prefer to use the phrase 'motivated commitment' instead of 'genuine commitment'. In our view, there are many situations where this willingness and enthusiasm are vital to the effective performance of the delegated task.

We view 'acceptance', as a somewhat grudging agreement that they will try to perform the task. The impression you get here is that they feel they HAVE to do it, but show little enthusiasm.

HOW DO YOU DECIDE WHETHER YOU NEED GENUINE COMMITMENT OR ACCEPTANCE?

Often it is not easy. Sometimes it is very clear-cut, but occasionally it is hard to be certain. We have listed below a number of delegation situations. Read through each and decide whether genuine commitment from the delegatee or just acceptance is needed, and why. There is some space after the situations for you to note down your thoughts.

Situation 1 A manager has identified development growth potential in one of her team members. She knows that the person concerned is keen to progress in the organisation, and has commitments at home as well (looking after an ageing father). She plans to delegate the task of preparing the development plan to the team member. In addition to other things, the plan will identify the most appropriate methods of training to meet the identified skills and knowledge needs. Various options are available including formal short courses, on-job coaching, and/or an Open University type course involving work in own time.

135

Situation 2 The Head Groom of a medium-sized stable is looking forward to an important showing event that will take place over the coming weekend. The owner of the stable has just phoned to say that she has entered a team in the driving event due to a last minute withdrawal. The Head Groom would normally prepare the show harnesses for the driving team but must spend the next two days until the show schooling the horses, otherwise they will not be ready. The groom needs to delegate the preparation of the harnesses which are filthy but need to look pristine. The problem is that the only stable girl available is covering for the others who are helping at the show ground. She's feeling left out anyway and is not likely to exactly welcome the extra work with open arms.

Situation 3 The Secretary of a local charity has to delegate the task of persuading the local council to support a forthcoming fund-raising event by providing exclusive use of the town swimming pool for a day at no cost. The Secretary will be away on (immovable) business on the date set for the Council's evening meeting. At the last appraisal, two weeks ago, the delegatee expressed a wish for 'a bit of a challenge now and then'. The delegatee has plenty of creative ideas but does not have very much 'selling' experience . . . and a couple of the more influential Council members will not be easily persuaded.

Situation 4 The manager of a large department store has just been asked, by the Managing Director, to prepare and present the quarterly figures for the store at the next shareholders' meeting. This meeting will consist of seven people; four shareholders and three directors who are also shareholders. During the conversation, the Store Manager explained that he will be speaking (as the main guest) at a merchandising conference on the day of the shareholders' meeting so would be unable to attend in person. The MD understood but stated that the presentation must take place on that day, so the Store Manager must delegate the task. His deputy would normally 'stand-in' but is on maternity leave and will not return in time. The manager has enough time to prepare the figures but the task of actually presenting them will have to be delegated to one of the members of the team. The person chosen by the manager understands the format for these figures and has made a number of fairly informal presentations to people within the store before. However they are known to lack confidence in their ability to make effective presentations to more formal groups. No one else in the team could handle this task.

Decide whether each situation requires commitment or acceptance, and why?

_____

_____

_____

_____

_____

_____

_____

Our view on these situations, and why

You may have gone one step further and thought about how you might actually handle each situation, so we have also added a few thoughts on that as well.

Situation 1 Genuine commitment is needed, and the person is halfway there already. They are 'keen to learn and want to progress'. Their genuine commitment is vital to the training plan if it is to be effective and because it is likely to have an impact both at work and at home. By enabling the person to select the training methods, they will be able to choose the method that meets the need, suits their way of learning, and is manageable considering the commitments. They will need to feel a personal responsibility for the plan, i.e. 'own' it, so grudging acceptance is not enough to make it work.

Providing the recommendations made by the delegatee meet the training needs and are feasible, we would accept them as they stand.

Situation 2 Realistically, only acceptance is needed here. The task is fairly routine, and the delegatee is already feeling rather like 'Cinderella' so there is no way the groom is likely to achieve willing enthusiasm from her.

The groom would need to explain why the task is needed in time for the show and why she needs to do it. With the other work she has to do, she is not going to like it but there is no other choice. If she does a good job, we would probably try hard to *ensure* that she went to the next show but would *not* mention that now in case something arose that made it impossible at the time. Assuming that it is feasible at the time, we would tell her why then.

Situation 3 Genuine commitment is needed; acceptance of the need to do it would not be enough. The person is looking for 'a bit of a challenge'. This task would represent just that, but they will need to feel that it is *realistic*. The delegatee has some 'selling' experience, but may well doubt their ability to handle this particular situation. To make an *effective* 'selling' presentation to the Council would require, in our view, genuine commitment; the person needs to believe that they can handle it, and want to handle it.

The person's creativity could be brought into play to identify ways of giving impact to the presentation. They have some experience but a 'dummy-run' with questions, or just practise on question handling, might increase their confidence by proving that they can cope with this challenge.

Situation 4 This is a tricky one; borderline 'commitment'. The person understands the format of the figures and has made presentations before. You might say that 'acceptance' is enough as the presentation *has* to take place on that day and the delegatee is the only person who could potentially cope. There is no other choice available. Secondly the person is only 'presenting the figures' so may not have to handle the sorts of questions that would be asked of the Store Manager.

However, the need for 'genuine commitment' is indicated by the person's lack of confidence in their ability to handle more formal presentations. No one will benefit if they 'go to pieces'! Although this is a smallish group, it is a very senior group, and, life being as it is, they *might* just ask some tough questions, and expect answers! If the delegatee has only given grudging acceptance, it is very likely to show at this point . . . 'Sorry, I don't know that. I'm only a 'stand-in' after all'.

This needs very careful handling by the Store Manager. The first objective has to be to obtain acceptance. However, we would try to obtain commitment to whatever extent is possible, using knowledge of the figures and previous presentations as proof of ability. Help the person build up their confidence by asking them to suggest actions that might make them feel more comfortable about making the presentation, and then respond accordingly. It *might* be possible for the Store Manager to agree with the MD that any questions concerning the actual management of the store could be held until his return from the conference, if that's what the delegatee wants.

So, in summary, when deciding whether genuine commitment is needed or acceptance is sufficient, the key factors that should be considered are as follows. You need **genuine commitment** from the delegatee when:

- They will view the task as a challenge. For example, making decisions on your behalf.

- The task is developmental (within the job, or for promotion); enabling them to develop or extend their skills/knowledge.

- You are delegating the task to order to motivate them; to provide more interesting work, for example.

- They must really *want* to do it in order to succeed. For example, where they may have used some of their own personal time to complete the task.

You only need **acceptance** when:

- The task is straightforward for them and will be seen as boring or mundane. For example, you are producing the text for a report and ask them to collate and total the figures for you, to meet the deadline.

- Where there is *no other choice* but to use that particular person on that task, although they would not normally be the one you would choose, (but don't expect the level of performance that you would get from someone with commitment). A crisis of some sort can often produce this type of situation. Say that you urgently need some data from the computer whilst you do something else. The only other person there might be the least experienced with the computer so will take significantly longer to extract the information that you need.

A general point to remember is that the person must have the ability to do the task, otherwise it will be seen as an impossibility.

There are numerous delegation situations where willingness and enthusiasm are absolutely vital if the task is to be performed successfully. How effective would a deputy be, without a willingness to take on the role and a degree of enthusiasm for it? Some managers, however, seem to try and obtain genuine commitment *every time*, because they believe this is the right way to operate with people. Whilst laudable, they are setting an unrealistic target for themselves; rather like expecting your eighteen-year-old son to be in by 10pm every night. As you will have seen from this section, you simply cannot expect to get 'genuine commitment', in the way we have defined it, every time!

139

> **Don't strive for *commitment* when all you can realistically expect (or need), is *acceptance***

As we have already said, there are many situations where genuine commitment *is* needed so we will now look at how to go about actually obtaining it.

How do you obtain this genuine commitment?

Before we go through our ideas, list down your thoughts on this question from your own experiences; either delegating or being on the receiving end.

_____

_____

_____

Earlier we described 'genuine commitment' as a willing agreement by the delegatee to carry out the task to the best of their ability. You have the impression that they really WANT to do it, and are enthusiastic about it. You could also term this as 'motivated'; the process of motivation gets them there. We believe that there are four guidelines that help in obtaining genuine commitment (or motivating them to reach that level, if you prefer). These guidelines are:

- having realistic expectations
- involving them in the whole process
- showing that minor mistakes will be accepted
- helping identify the benefits to *them* of doing the task
- if you are delegating to improve motivation, ensure that you *really* know what motivates that person.

HAVING REALISTIC EXPECTATIONS

Let's say that you have selected the task and the person to whom it can be delegated. You have arrived at that point by deciding that any skill or knowledge gaps can be effectively handled in some way. You see your expectations as realistic because you believe that the person already has, or can develop, the ability to carry out the task successfully. The problem is that the person might not believe you!

In the previous chapter, we looked at how to show our confidence in the person's ability during the delegation discussion by proving they had the ability. Remember that you, as manager, might view something as a 'challenge' but if they see it as an 'impossibility' then you will not get commitment. If the person has some prior experiences that enable you to do this, that's fine. This is not always possible, in terms of hard fact anyway. Occasionally, you might be relying on your judgement (or gut-feel if you like) rather than on hard fact. Facts can't be wrong but judgement can. Does that mean then that your expectations might be unrealistic? Maybe, but not necessarily. To answer this, talk to the person concerned about why you believe they can handle it, why you feel as you do, and resolve any concerns that they have.

When I was in my twenties, I was running one of two sections in a department of a large engineering firm. My boss was off on a two-week training course and needed a 'stand-in'. The obvious choice was one of the two section leaders. I had been a section leader for far less time than my colleague but he was incredibly busy at that particular point in the financial year. So, with his okay, our boss asked me to 'stand in'. I like to think I was doing a reasonable job as a section leader, but I had never 'stood in' for my boss before. There were no examples of 'standing in' that he could use to actually *prove* that I could handle the role. What he did do was very clever, and typical of him. Early in the discussion I suppose I questioned 'the realism of his expectation'. He talked about a number of different issues that could arise (including one where an unpopular decision would have to be made) and asked me how I would handle them. I don't pretend that I had all of the right answers because I didn't, but he built up my confidence to a point where I thought I might just cope with it, even though I had never done it before. In other words, I came to believe that the expectation was just about realistic (and maybe my responses might have confirmed it in his own mind; I'm not sure). Afterwards we had a review. (Yes, the unpopular decision HAD arisen.) Whilst some things could certainly have been improved or better handled, the outcome was *'Right. As you didn't actually make the firm bankrupt, I see no reason why you can't stand in for me again. Thanks for doing it.'*

INVOLVING THEM IN THE WHOLE PROCESS, AND WHAT NOT TO DO

141

There is, it seems, a strong link between commitment and involvement; the more you involve a person, the more they are likely to feel committed to the outcome. In other words, they 'own' it.

In the last chapter on 'Handling the delegation discussion', we talked about involvement and the importance of effective questions. These questions encourage, probe, and clarify the delegatee's views steering them to meet the objective that you have set for the discussion. Providing that you actually *use* their input, then commitment to, and ownership of, the plan is very likely.

The last point about actually using their input is important; some managers ask for ideas then ignore them!

Avoid pseudo-democracy

'Pseudo-democracy' is asking for suggestions, getting workable ones, and then doing something entirely different ... because the decision was already made. 'Karen, how do you think we could do that?' 'Well, I think that we really need to deal with this face-to-face, Peter.' 'That's a terrific idea, Karen, but I had already decided that we will send him a letter.' (If you have encountered it at some time or another, you will know exactly how it feels!)

There is a slightly different situation that can occur and it *feels* much like 'pseudo-democracy'. Sometimes managers seem to confuse 'involvement' with 'consultation'; they believe that they are involving but, in fact, are actually consulting. For example, 'I'll find out how he thinks we should do this then I will decide the best way forward' (consultation). The delegatee however sees it as 'I'm being asked for my view so he's bound to use it. He wouldn't ask if not' (involvement).

If you are trying to get commitment through involvement, you must be prepared to *use* their ideas providing, of course, they are workable ideas. If a suggestion is basically sound but has one aspect that would cause problems, explain that you like the overall idea, and why you have a concern about one element, then ask for solutions. If they can't provide any, perhaps they will ask for your thoughts. They are still genuinely involved; they just chose to involve you as well because they didn't have the answer needed. Even though it is not their idea, there is still likely to be commitment because they were given the chance but could not provide the answer.

Do you always need involvement to obtain commitment?

No, not always! Willing and enthusiastic agreement to carry out a task can still result from a straightforward explanation of the requirements and the reasons underlying the choices. Suppose that you have a deputy who has successfully 'stood in' to chair meetings for you on numerous occasions in the past, i.e. they are at level 4. You are about to ask them to do so again. Do you really need very much involvement to get commitment? They are 'comfortable' and KNOW they can handle it. Apart from a brief check, probably not. You just explain what is required and why, ensure that it is feasible, check they are still 'comfortable', then let them get on with it. Five minutes, at most! All the involvement necessary has gone before, genuine commitment has been obtained already.

There is another type of situation where involvement is not necessary for commitment. If they have only limited, or no knowledge but see you as an expert, they probably expect you to explain what to do and how to do it. They are happy (committed) to do it YOUR way, because they believe you know what you are doing and presumably trust you. In fact, if you tried to ask them what they would do, they may not be able to give you any useful input. As their experience grows, the situation changes. More involvement would be needed to gain the necessary commitment because they now have their own opinions as to what and what not to do.

Ensure that the output from involvement will actually produce the results you need

Some managers in their quest for commitment through involvement can lose sight of the overall requirements. This point is illustrated in the following example.

A revised computer program to produce management reports on cash flow had been recently installed in the regional office of a public utility organisation. The revision only changed the format of the reports so that data was shown in a clearer way. At lunch-time the Senior Programmer responsible for installing the revision received a call from the finance people saying that there was a problem with the revised program as some of the cash flow reports were coming out incorrectly printed (portrait instead of landscape, so information was all over the place). This needed rectification quickly as the senior managers were meeting at 4pm to go over the monthly figures. Due to the urgency, the Senior Programmer would normally have dealt with this personally but had prior urgent and important programming commitments, so needed to delegate it. One of his programmers was very good at fixing 'bugs' so he was called in and the problem was explained. The programmer had one or two concerns because of unfamiliarity with that revision and the conversation became very technical. The involvement generated various interesting ideas and a fairly complex plan was produced which had the total commitment of the programmer.

At ten minutes past four, the Head of Finance rang the Senior Programmer asking about the reports. *'Sorry. They should be there by now.'* Then, like a thunderbolt from the blue, realisation hit him! Downstairs he went, with a strong suspicion as to what had gone wrong. There was the programmer looking very pleased with himself; he had found the problem, and SIX other unrelated minor 'bugs', and had **decided to re-write the revision program!** He was having a whale of a time but it was nowhere near ready, and the original 'bug' was not yet fixed.

143

You have probably decided that there were many things wrong here (objective, controls, etc.) and we would agree. One of the main causes was that both had become so involved in the detail discussion that the result (enable the reports to be produced in time for the 4pm meeting by fixing the bug) had got lost. In the cold light of this book, most would say 'That should have been easy. Fix the bug, produce the reports, and *then* sort out the rest of the program, but this sort of thing happens. The Senior Programmer used involvement to remove the concerns expressed by the programmer, and the resulting plan certainly achieved commitment, but it was genuine commitment TO THE WRONG THING (at that point in time anyway). When this happens, we call it 'the smiling lemming syndrome'. **In other words, the person is totally committed (i.e. willing and enthusiastic) to a course of action that will completely fail to achieve the result required.**

SHOWING THAT MINOR MISTAKES WILL BE ACCEPTED

We have mentioned this in an earlier chapter but it is worth elaborating on the theme here as it can be a very significant factor when trying to obtain commitment. A 'minor mistake' to us, is one that does not adversely affect the result you are trying to achieve. For example, wasting five minutes in a presentation by going into too much detail might be a minor mistake, whereas failing to convince the audience would be major. The latter mistake has affected the result, whereas the former has not.

Few of us are likely to feel overly enthusiastic about a visit to the executioner's block, yet that is what some managers seem to expect. If you expect commitment (willingness and enthusiasm) from someone, you will *not* get it if, from past experience, they expect to get a telling-off at the end of the job. Unfortunately some people *say* that minor mistakes are okay, but when it comes down to it, minor mistakes are *not* accepted. If you *say* it, you must be prepared to *do* it! So how do you do it?

Put the point across in any way that suits your own style but the principle is, 'When anyone tries something new there are likely to be minor mistakes. Everyone does it. That's okay, I don't expect perfection. Try to do the best you can and let me know if you are concerned about anything. After the task is finished we will review it, see if there is anything that we think could have been improved and work out what to do next time'.

Back their decisions

Ask anyone who has been given delegated authority to make independent decisions for a guideline and we would suggest that 99 per cent will say something like 'The manager must actually back any decisions I make'.

A further aspect of genuinely showing that minor mistakes will be accepted is to back the person's decisions even if you would have acted differently. If you have given someone the authority to make independent decisions on your behalf, you trust their judgement but they may still make *minor* mistakes. For example, suppose they need to choose between four options; numbers one and two are close and would both work, three and four are a long way behind. They decide on number two, but you believe that number one would have been better had they looked more broadly at the criteria. We would class this as a minor mistake and believe that it is vital to support their choice even though you may discuss it afterwards to help them learn something for future use.

A manager (Fred) who we both know, was standing in for his director who was in the USA on business. Just prior to his departure, the director sent round a note saying:

> **MEMORANDUM**
>
> Fred will be standing in for me for the next two weeks whilst I am in the USA. Please note that he has my authority to make decisions on my behalf, throughout that period.
>
> Signed .... Production Director.

During the fortnight, a key machine broke down and the job that was currently on that machine was required urgently by the customer. The other two machines were fully occupied with urgent work also. Additional production costs had to be approved by the Production Director on an order of this value. Fred knew the Production Director's view that agreed delivery dates HAD to be met, so he rapidly arranged for the work to be sent to a good sub-contractor and it was completed and sent in time. On his return, the Production Director publicly supported Fred's decision totally and signed off the extra costs of sub-contracting when the invoice came in. However they had a *private* discussion in which Fred was asked what options he had considered other than sub-contracting.

145

'None if I'm honest. The other machines were fully occupied, and this order was urgent', said Fred.

'What about doing the work on one or two of the good machines over the intervening weekend?'

'You're right. That probably would have been cheaper than sub-contracting and it would still have met the deadline. Whoops!' replied a somewhat shamefaced Fred.

'Don't get worried. The bottom line is that you didn't just sit on the fence, and the customer got their order on time. In future, just remember to look at all of your options. '

How comfortable would *you* feel if you had to stand in for that director in the future?

Helping identify the benefits to *them* of doing the task

When delegating, most managers will cover the benefits to the department or organisation of doing the task. What we sometimes forget to do is to identify the *benefits to the person* whom we are going to ask to actually do the job. You cannot always do this because not all delegated tasks have a benefit to the delegatee, apart from, maybe, 'being seen as helpful by the boss'. Consider a situation where you just need someone to total up 20 pages of figures for you to save you time. The job will probably be seen as pretty boring with virtually no benefit to the delegatee. Don't try to invent one please. People spot it instantly.

Why bother? Aren't they obvious anyway?

Sometimes, but certainly not always obvious. Let's deal first with 'Why bother?'

An explanation of the benefits to the department or organisation is important and should be covered. However in this chapter, we are talking about how to obtain *commitment*. The premise is this. The more someone can see a personal benefit for doing something, the more they are likely to be committed to it, rather than simply accept the need to do it.

There are some very bright youngsters around who are very good at naturally doing this. For example, 'Daddy, if I can have that dress now (in September), it could be my Christmas present, couldn't it?' (Have you noticed how large their eyes get when they do this to you?) You agree, and buy the dress for her. She 'sold' you quite naturally on a benefit to YOU (avoiding one bit of expense at an expensive time) and got your commitment to it, (or was it just acceptance?).

Now the real question is . . . *what happens when you get to Christmas?* You know, don't you? and so do I! Parents stand no chance in the face of this.

Now for the 'Aren't they obvious?' question. When you prepared for the discussion, you probably identified what the benefit (or benefits) might be to the person of carrying out the task, e.g. helping with development, more interest via new skills in the present job, and so on. Strangely enough, some managers never seem to refer to these, presumably on the assumption either that it's obvious, or the person already knows. That is NOT always the case.

Commitment and involvement are linked so it is important to cover them by asking the person the benefits THEY see for themselves in doing the task and helping if they have missed anything significant. You may be really surprised how their interpretation of the situation and benefits can differ significantly from you own. It is particularly important when you are trying to obtain commitment to a 'developmental' task so that the person clearly appreciates how the task will help them. If you have had a prior discussion with them about their development needs, they should be able to identify the benefits without too much input from you.

IF YOU ARE DELEGATING TO IMPROVE MOTIVATION, ENSURE THAT YOU *REALLY* KNOW WHAT MOTIVATES THAT PERSON

Obtaining genuine commitment when using the task for motivational purposes is vital if the desired result is to stand any chance of being achieved. In order to do this, we need to establish what actually motivates the person and then select a task that will provide that motivational factor (or factors).

GETTING GENUINE COMMITMENT

The whole subject of 'motivation' is very complex and could easily occupy an entire book all on its own. The difficulty we had was deciding how much to cover to meet the objectives with regard to motivation and its place in delegation. What we have tried to do in this section is'to help you to think about what motivation really is, give you some thoughts on how you might find out what motivates someone, how you draw the links with the task you have selected, and how to obtain commitment in this situation.

What motivates you? Please list your thoughts below.

_____

_____

_____

_____

_____

Now, mentally identify a colleague and decide what you believe motivates that person.

_____

_____

_____

_____

Now write down your definition of 'motivation'.

_____

_____

_____

_____

_____

_____

_____

What is 'motivation'?

The first point to make is that you probably found this quite hard to define. Strangely enough, 'motivation' is one of those words that we use very frequently, but find difficult to actually define. A fairly common dictionary definition of motivation is 'that which provides an incentive to act'. The problem with this definition in a management or delegation sense, is that an incentive can be positive or negative. For example, fear is a negative incentive. If the fear is strong enough, it will certainly produce action! The question is whether that is the *right* sort of motive for someone carrying out a delegated task; we believe it is not.

Did your definition include any words such as 'willing', 'encourage', or 'help'? If so, you are seeing motivation in a positive sense, as we do.

> **Our definition of motivation:**
> **'encouraging someone to give their very best**
> **within their capabilities'**

The link between commitment and motivation

It is very easy to get thoroughly confused between 'commitment' and 'motivation'. The way we separate them is to view 'motivation' as encouraging them to actually *give their very best* to the task, and 'commitment' as a willing *agreement* by the delegatee to carry out the task to the best of their ability. In other words, in order to get a genuine commitment from the person to whom you are delegating, we believe that the person must be motivated. Obviously that motivation also needs to be maintained throughout performance of the task.

How do you actually find out what motivates someone?

The worst thing to do is actually say to someone, 'What motivates you?', as we did at the start of this section. (This was done on purpose, by the way.) It *sounds* a simple question, but is extremely complex and difficult to answer. Due to this complexity, many people tend to give fairly straightforward, easy to identify answers, i.e. money, better car, promotion, etc. If we had said, 'what makes you tick?' you may well have found that a far more difficult question to answer, but that is really what we are trying to find out when asking someone about motivation.

Suppose we try a slightly different question. What do you enjoy doing (at work), and why? Then rank (high, medium, or low) these reasons in terms of importance to you, i.e. the extent to which that factor encourages you to give the best of which you are capable.

_____

_____

_____

_____

_____

_____

When doing this, you might also identify that some factor (or factors) seems to be a 'keynote' for you, e.g. everything that you really enjoy has an element of challenge and sense of achievement.

149

Did you find this question easier or more difficult to answer than the 'what motivates you?' question? Ask yourself which question ('what motivates you?' or 'what do you enjoy doing?') told you more about the factors that motivate you. The answers to the latter question seem to provide much more useful information on what _really_ motivates someone at work. There appears to be a link between enjoyment and motivation. Having said that, it is somewhat of a 'chicken and egg' situation. We don't know which comes first. Is someone motivated because they enjoy the task, or do they enjoy it because they are motivated? Draw your own conclusions and see if you agree.

At this point it is worth looking at an aspect of one of the main motivation theories that we find extremely useful when trying to identify the factors that motivate an individual. Frederick Hertzberg investigated the factors that affect job attitudes. He then identified those factors that lead to satisfaction and dissatisfaction at work. We do not intend to review his entire theory here; it has been well documented already. If you have not encountered it before you may find it makes interesting and useful reading.

In looking at motivation and its place in delegation, we will concentrate on those factors that lead to 'satisfaction'; the 'motivators' as Hertzberg called them. The list that follows is based on Hertzberg's list of motivators but we have made some modifications and separated some of them simply because, over the years, we have found it beneficial to do so when trying to identify and record what motivates an individual.

Motivating factors (in alphabetical order):

- achievement, i.e. doing what you set out to do
- challenge
- clear realistic objectives
- interesting work
- objective-balanced feedback on your performance
- opportunity for promotion/advancement
- opportunity to develop skills and knowledge
- recognition by others
  responsibility (and trust).

In order to test the value of this list, look back at the reasons you wrote down in response to the earlier question 'what do you enjoy doing at work, and why?' The actual words might differ somewhat but are your reasons broadly covered in this list? If so, then you might like to consider using the list as a way of recording the factors that motivate people in your team. We will explain how later.

If there are differences between your reasons and the factors we have included in the list, then consider whether modifications or additions to the list would enable you to use it with your people.

Let's now deal with the last aspect of your work in this section. Earlier we asked you to list the factors that you believe motivate a colleague. Were they significantly different from those factors that apply to you? Some of these factors seem to apply to most people but their importance can vary dramatically. For example, you and I might both be motivated by being given responsibility, but it may be the most important factor for you yet be third on my list.

Secondly, how sure are you that you have *correctly* identified the factors that motivate that person? Most people seem to be uncertain, but your answer will depend on how well you know that person already. You are possibly thinking, *How do I know unless I actually ask them?* That's exactly our point!

Sadly, rather than try to find out what someone actually enjoys doing, some managers assume that they genuinely know.

The manager thinks, *Dave is retiring next year. He won't want the extra responsibility that goes with this project.*

Dave however thinks, *Hope I get that new project. With my experience I've done most things and this is new. I could really use a bit of a challenge to fire me up.*

> **To find out what motivates someone, don't make assumptions! Try asking them, 'What do you enjoy doing (at work), and why?'**

If you like the idea of using this question with people in your team, consider recording the results (after the discussion) on your own modified version of a Motivation Factors form. List the factors down the left-hand side, then add columns across the page for each member of your team. As we said earlier, the ranking of the factors is likely to differ between individuals. Once you have the factors in your mind, you will spot them as the conversation progresses. For example:

'What do you enjoy doing, and why?'
   'I enjoyed doing that project last month. It was brand new and nobody had tried to do anything like that before.' ('challenge', you think)
   'Anything else?'
   'Yes, there was actually. I wasn't sure that I could handle it but I got a real buzz when it was finished (achievement) *and what was nice was that you put my name on the front cover of the report.'* (recognition)
   'Which of those things were most important to you, do you think?'
   'Well ... probably the feeling that I had finished everything one week ahead of the deadline.' (If you are ranking, then this comment tells you that 'Achievement' is certainly a 'high' for that person.)

After the meeting, you can enter either 'ticks' or some form of ranking (H, M, L) on the form. It is also important to remember that, whilst the factors MAY stay relatively constant over time for a person, the ranking may change over the months or years. For example, the most important factor for someone with only six months' experience might be 'achievement'; after two years, the most important might be 'challenge' because they know by now that they can 'achieve'. 'Achievement' has not disappeared, it has just moved down their list. If you do decide to keep a list then try to remember to review it periodically, say, once a year.

Whilst this question is useful if you are trying to identify tasks for delegation that will motivate, it can also be used generally to find out the things that are important to *all* members of your team, not just those to whom you might delegate.

How do you draw the links between these motivational factors and the task you have selected?

Having identified the factors, it is *vital* that you check your understanding/perceptions with the person concerned, i.e. *'From what you have said, it seems to me that a sense of achievement is important to you. Is that right?'* Vital, because an incorrect interpretation and so the wrong choice of task, is likely to *demotivate*. Not very helpful!

Assuming that you have correctly interpreted their views, you can then consider their skills and knowledge and the tasks you do, and decide which task(s) are:

■ within their capabilities,

and

■ will provide the motivation factors that you have jointly identified.

When you meet to brief them for the task, a link back to your earlier discussion with a brief summary of the key points/factors should enable you to explain why you are about to ask them to carry out this task.

'Kate, when we last spoke you explained that you feel there is not much challenge for you at the moment and that you are looking for an opportunity to develop within your present job. So I would like to ask you to carry out a job for me that I hope will help on both counts. You are very good on internal presentations and I think you are ready to handle some to customers. They are not easy but I am sure you will be able to use your existing skills in that area.'

How do you obtain commitment in this situation?

'Commitment' is willing, enthusiastic agreement to carry out the task. During the discussion, ensure that they are genuinely seeing the task as a challenge, not as an impossibility. Secondly, your objective is to motivate, so 'acceptance' is not enough. Watch reactions throughout your briefing and, where possible, get them to identify the benefits of carrying out the task. Pose 'open' questions, such as; 'What sort of challenge do you feel that will present, Mark?' or 'In what way do you think that task will help you develop towards a management role?'

Helping them to link the task you are delegating to the factors that are important to them, should produce motivation. If not, something has been missed or misinterpreted.

At the end of the discussion, ask them how they actually feel about doing the task. This should tell you whether you have genuine commitment. Remember that grudging 'acceptance' is not enough.

What if, despite your hard work, you don't actually *get* commitment?

Suppose you reach the end of the discussion, and receive replies such as: 'Sorry, boss. I'm not at all happy. I really do not want to do that', or perhaps, 'I suppose I'll *have* to do it, if you insist.'

One way might be to say, 'Tough luck, pal. Do it anyway!', but this doesn't really do very much to help in obtaining *commitment*.

There are basically three options open to you, at this point.

- Conclude that you are *not* going to get the commitment necessary to carry out the task successfully, and stop there.

- Decide that 'commitment' is unrealistic or unnecessary, and something slightly better than 'acceptance' is adequate.

- Find out what went wrong, go back to the start, and try again to get the commitment you need.

CONCLUDE THAT YOU ARE *NOT* GOING TO GET THE COMMITMENT NECESSARY TO CARRY OUT THE TASK SUCCESSFULLY, AND STOP THERE

This is always a difficult option (from both viewpoints). You feel that you have failed to get the necessary commitment, when you believed that you should have been able to obtain it. The person to whom you were trying to delegate may well feel that they have let you down.

Before you decide to 'stop it there', be absolutely sure that genuine 'commitment' is VITAL if the task is to be successfully completed, and that you are definitely NOT going to get the commitment required. In your preparation, you may have misjudged the situation. If you now decide that 'acceptance' is enough, you do not need to stop. (The next section suggests some ideas to help with this.) Alternatively, you may not have handled the discussion as well as you might have hoped. If you feel that you CAN get commitment, a lot more work will be needed. (The final section provides some guidance.)

Let's take the worst case. Commitment is vital, and there is no way that you are going to get it, so you decide to stop it there. The first point to make is that this is better than forcing someone into a situation in which they are likely to fail, and for which you are accountable as well. Everyone loses!

The question is how do you 'stop it there' without too much damage, on either side. Both of you may be feeling concerned at this point. You presumably didn't expect them to react as they have and they are wondering what the effect of their actions might be.

If possible, try to jointly arrive at the decision to abandon. You might think, *Why not let **them** make the decision?* Understandable, but ask yourself how they are going to feel about that afterwards. The plus point is that they will 'own' the decision, but the minus point is that they may unjustly blame themselves for the situation. It may not have been their fault that the situation arose; it might be that you misjudged their ability or feelings so the fault is really yours, not theirs. If this is the case, it may be worth saying so. Use your own approach/words but, as an example:

'Steve, I thought that this would represent a challenge for you but I was wrong. I am asking too much of you considering your present level of knowledge. That's my fault, not yours. In a few months when you have more experience, we could look at opportunities for doing this job then. What do you think?'

Try putting yourself in the delegatee's position. How would you feel about a statement like this? Our example also illustrates another important point; **show them that this particular situation has not removed all future opportunities**. In a situation like this, most people will wonder about the future and what effect their action might have. They rarely seem to actually ask the question but it is in their mind. It makes sense to answer it.

DECIDE THAT 'COMMITMENT' IS UNREALISTIC, AND SOMETHING SLIGHTLY BETTER THAN 'ACCEPTANCE' IS ADEQUATE

During your preparation, you decided that commitment (a willing, enthusiastic agreement to carry out the task) would be necessary. In the course of your discussion, however, it becomes clear that all you can realistically expect is 'acceptance plus', i.e. he or she is willing enough, but they won't really be enthusiastic until they have actually done some of it, and know that they will succeed.

An example might help to illustrate such a situation.

A departmental manager was asked by the Training Department to act as a guest speaker on the next internal training course, which both she and a member of her team had previously attended. The manager was unable to attend but, with the full support of the Training Department, delegated the job to the team member. The team member was very competent at presentations and extremely knowledgeable on the topic concerned. However, that person had never been involved in training before except as a course attendee so was understandably concerned. On the one hand they felt it was nice to be asked to stand in for the manager like this; on the other hand they were concerned in case it went wrong. The manager and team member jointly produced a plan that included a dummy-run to the manager and the rest of the team, prior to speaking on the course. The manager realised that to expect enthusiasm at the planning stage was rather unrealistic as the person was unsure about their ability to cope. (They were quite willing to 'give it a go'.) It is fairly unlikely that much would change in this respect until the person had run a successful mock training session with the manager and team. The manager realised that a successful dummy-run should generate the enthusiasm needed to make the 'real' training session work.

Enthusiasm may be necessary for the final phase of the task but may not realistically be generated until some of the work has been successfully completed.

FIND OUT WHAT WENT WRONG, GO BACK TO THE START, AND TRY AGAIN TO GET THE COMMITMENT YOU NEED

Despite your earlier efforts, they are not convinced (yet) and you may have to start again. Please do not do what some people manage to do; go back to the start and hope that repetition of everything solves it. It can sound almost like a tape recording of the first discussion. Have you ever watched someone trying to give directions to a stranger who does not speak the local language well or at all? Firstly they SHOUT, and they keep repeating the same thing time after time, as if that is going to make it any clearer to the poor lost soul!

155

The important thing before you try again is to think about WHY you have not got the commitment that you need. A few of the possible reasons are:

■ They might feel that they are facing an impossibility, rather than a challenge, because you have not adequately proved to them that they have the necessary ability.

■ They may not understand (or have forgotten) why you have selected them for the task.

■ They might be covering themselves in case it goes wrong, e.g. 'Well, I only said I'd try because you insisted. I wasn't sure that I could do it. It's not my fault it went wrong.'

You can probably think of additional possible reasons for this reaction.

HOW DO YOU DEAL WITH IT?

Don't guess! Try to identify the reason(s) with their help, and ensure that you fully understand them before moving on.

Having got to that point, involve them in identifying what can be done to resolve the issue(s). Try and avoid the tendency to provide all of the answers yourself. You are only trying to help but remember that commitment and involvement are closely linked. Just because you give me, as the delegatee, an answer to a concern that I have, does not mean that I believe you. Mum to daughter; 'You won't be late back from that party tonight, will you?' and gets, 'Course not, Mum!' It's now 2am and . . .

A further point on this is that *your* way of solving that issue, however well meant, may not be how *I* want to solve it. Encourage them to suggest ways of resolving their concerns.

SUMMARY – CHAPTER 9

■ 'Genuine commitment' is a willing, enthusiastic agreement to carry out the task to the best of that person's ability

■ Don't try for 'genuine commitment' when you can only realistically expect 'acceptance', e.g. boring task

■ How to obtain genuine commitment:
 – Ensure your expectations are realistic
 – Involve them int he whole process
 – Show that minor mistakes will be accepted
 – Help to identify the benefits to *them* of carrying out the task
 – If delegating to improve motivation, ensure that you *really* know what motivates that person.

■ Realistic expectations:
 – Explain why you think they can handle the task
 – Why you feel as you do (to explain things that you can't prove)
 – Resolve any concerns that they may have.

■ Involve them in the whole process:
 – There seems to be a strong link between involvement and commitment
 – Avoid 'pseudo-democracy', i.e. **pretending** to involve them
 – Watch out for 'Smiling Lemmings'
 – Be prepared to actually **back** their decisions!

■ Helping to identify the benefits to **them** of doing the task:·
 – If there are **no** benefits, don't try to invent them!
 – Ask **them** what they see as the benefits of doing the task.

■ If delegating to improve motivation, ensure that you really know what motivates them:
 – Motivation should be positive (encouragement), rather than negative (fear)
 – Ask them 'What do you enjoy doing (at work), and why?'
 – Don't assume that you know the answers to the previous question
 – When choosing the task, ensure it is within their capabilities and provides the motivation factors you have jointly identified
 – At the end of the discussion, check how they feel about doing the task.

■ What if you don't get the commitment that you need? Three options:
 – If you decide to stop it there, try to jointly arrive at the decision to abandon it, and show that it has not removed future opportunities.

157

- You might decide that 'commitment' is unrealistic, and something slightly better than acceptance is adequate i.e. when enthusiasm will only be generated after some of the work has been successfully completed.
- Find out what went wrong, and try again. Identify the reasons for lack of commitment with their help and involve them in identifying what can be done to resolve the concerns.

10

Control without interference

Overview of this chapter

As the title of this book is 'Letting Go Without Losing Control', this particular chapter is extremely important. Deciding on, and maintaining an appropriate level of control is vital to ensure that the required result is achieved. In the section of Chapter 4, 'Won't I lose control?', we referred to the need to avoid over-control. The difficulty is to avoid what appears to be seen as 'management interference' (Long John Silver's parrot).

So the question is, 'How *do* you ensure adequate control without interference?' That question will be answered in this chapter. In addition to understanding the requirements of an effective control system, the 'trick' if you can call it that, is to **involve the delegatee in the whole process of control!**

What are the objectives for this chapter?

When you have read this chapter, you should:

■ know what a 'control' system should do, and how to do it
■ know how to involve the delegatee in the whole process of control to reduce the likelihood of perceived 'management interference'.

What is covered in this chapter?

■ What is 'control'?
■ What is a 'control' system?
■ How to involve the person so that the control system works well without perceived 'interference' from the manager?
■ The follow-up meeting; its importance and how to run it.

What is 'control'?

Please write down your definition of 'control' (within the context of delegation), followed by a brief outline of what you believe an effective 'control' system should contain.

OUR DEFINITION OF 'CONTROL'

We see it as 'monitoring the performance of the delegated task so that the expected results are successfully achieved'. This does not imply that the only person who can 'control' is the manager. Whereas the manager needs to maintain overall control of the task (otherwise it is abdication), the person to whom the task is delegated can often effectively identify and operate the day-to-day controls.

What is a 'control' system?

Just knowing what 'control' is does not help someone actually do it. What is needed is some form of process or system that outlines the steps or stages that need to be followed as illustrated in Figure 10.1.

An effective control system should:

■ identify what *should* happen

■ monitor the *actual* progress of the work

■ identify any significant *variation,* between what *should* happen and what *is* happening

■ and prompt the need for timely *corrective* action to ensure that the expected results are achieved

---

The difficulty for some people is that they tend to view control systems as something very 'formal'. In reality, we all use 'control systems' every day without sometimes actually realising it. For example, drivers will often listen to radio stations that give out regular traffic news so that, in the event of a traffic hold-up ahead, they can detour and still arrive at their destination on time (or close to it, at least).

Most people keep some form of 'To Do' list. It is one of the commonest forms of control system. You might like to briefly think about your own 'To Do' system and see how it compares with the steps we have listed above.

Before moving on to look at what is involved in each of these steps in detail, look back at the last activity and see if your views regarding the 'control' definition and control system differ significantly.

_____

_____

_____

_____

_____

_____

Plan	Checkpoints
Prepare draft outline of presentation.	By 14 September.
	15 minutes to cover objective, proposal, and benefits.
	Agree outline with manager on 15 September.
Dummy run of presentation to own team at Departmental meeting.	On 20 September.
	Make 15 minute presentation clear and concise, and use overhead transparencies (expected by customer). Effectively handle 'tough' questions from team (after the presentation).
Finalise presentation.	By 24 September.
	Ensure any points from the dummy run are included.
	Review with manager on 25 September.
Deliver presentation to customer.	On 26 September at 10am.
	Resolve any concerns and get agreement to proposal.
Review outcome with manager.	On 3 October.
	Discuss a summary of the discussion, questions raised and final outcome.

Fig 10.1 Sample plan for presentation

WHAT *SHOULD* HAPPEN

This first step of the control system identifies what should happen. The idea here is *not* to highlight everything! Identify the KEY ACTIVITIES only, i.e. those which, if a problem arises, will affect the overall result. If you have moved house at some stage, you will know that there seem to be hundreds of things you need to do in order to make the move successful. However, whilst they may all be desirable, only a relatively few activities are '**KEY**'. For example, it may not be a disaster if you forget to tell the photographic club to which you belong that you have moved until a couple of weeks after the event, but forgetting to arrange for the release of the new house keys is likely to be a disaster.

At this stage, you need to identify those things that should or must happen to ensure that the results you need are achieved. It is important to bear in mind that you are identifying what needs to happen, not how it should be done. From these tasks/activities, it is then possible to identify 'checkpoints'; progress/quality checks prior to critical steps in the plan which, if they fail, would produce a disaster.

With delegated tasks, the checkpoints should clearly indicate the deadlines and quality standards. So, for example, the plan and checkpoints for the preparation and delivery of a presentation to a major customer might look something like the plan below.

163

WHAT IS *ACTUALLY* HAPPENING

This step of the control system monitors what is actually happening. The frequency of monitoring what is going on is very important, particularly with longer-term elements of the delegation plan. For example, it would not be very much use looking at a 'To Do' list every month if all of the tasks on it had weekly deadlines.

When the day-to-day monitoring is to be done by the delegatee, they may need some guidance (or a reminder) as to the best approach to use, especially if they last did the task some time ago. A note for themselves (of deadlines and checkpoints) in their own diary is often all that is necessary.

IDENTIFYING ANY *SIGNIFICANT VARIATION* BETWEEN THE TWO

A good control system not only monitors what is going on; it highlights whether there is any significant variation between what should happen and what is happening. The key word is '**significant**'!

Ask yourself what you do when your bank statement arrives? Our bet is that the first place you look is the 'final balance'. In other words, 'Am I still solvent, or am I broke?' A few pounds here or there may not matter but if the final figure has a couple of zeros, *that* is significant!

With delegated tasks, it should be possible to identify whether there is a significant variation by looking at the checkpoints. Using the earlier example, if the dummy-run presentation to the team took 30 minutes, that is significant. If the presenter found one or two of the minor questions difficult to answer, that would probably not be a *significant* variation; nobody would handle every question perfectly.

PROMPT THE NEED FOR *TIMELY, CORRECTIVE* ACTION

In the event of a significant variation between what should happen and what is happening, timely corrective action puts the task back on track so that the result is achieved. Let's deal first with 'TIMELY'.

> **Ensure that the control system is not just a *management history book!***

Sadly, some so-called control systems are no more than management history books. Have you ever received a report that told you things had gone wrong one month after the event? As a control, they are useless because that bit of paper did not prompt timely action.

That really brings us on to a related point; the best control systems are often the simplest. Just to date us, many years ago, if your bank account was overdrawn you would get a statement *immediately* and, so that you didn't miss it, the bank also used to show the balance in red ink. The detail in the statement may only be useful if you need to find out where it all went. The red ink, and the fact that you received the bank statement at an unusual time, was a very effective, and simple control. It had the ability to prompt corrective action rather urgently! Going one stage further, you might be thinking that the situation shouldn't have really arisen in the first place. Agreed, but life being what it is, this sort of thing can happen. How many of us actually know at any point in time exactly how much we have in the account (or on our credit card); we know we *should* keep a check on it but often don't. That is where corrective action is so important.

Now for 'CORRECTIVE', in our earlier definition. It may be worth briefly explaining the difference between corrective action and interim action. Corrective action attacks the cause of the problem whereas, interim action deals with the effect. So, to stay with the overdrawn bank account example, corrective action would be aimed at what caused the account to become overdrawn. Interim action deals with the effect so you might transfer some cash from a deposit account to return the account to credit.

> **CORRECTIVE ACTION deals with the *cause*, to remove it, or at least reduce the chance of it recurring.**
>
> **INTERIM ACTION tackles the *effect*, by reducing the impact.**
>
> **Sadly, some people only ever seem to take interim actions!**

We have mentioned 'fire fighting' and 'fire prevention' before (in Chapter 6) but it is worth elaborating on their role here under 'Control'. Many years ago now, when the difference between them was first explained to me by my boss, it really hit home! I had tended to think of action as just action before; I had not separated them. I very quickly realised that the plus was that I was action-oriented; however the minus was that most of my actions were interim, i.e. 'fire fighting'. Sometimes we need someone else to show us things like that.

165

Unfortunately, some managers also seem only to take interim actions, i.e. 'fire fighting', whereas a corrective action might just prevent a fire from starting again in the future. The corrective action might just take a bit more time and thought, but it is worth it.

Sometimes you may need to take both forms of action. However it is important to remember that 'interim' action is only a holding action. It is 'corrective' action that corrects things longer term, by trying to remove the cause of the variation.

Returning to our 'presentation' example, the reviews and the dummy-run would allow for timely, corrective action to be taken, if required, prior to the actual presentation to the customer.

> **To provide effective control but avoid the perception of management 'interference', *involve the delegatee in the whole process of control*, when possible.**

How to involve the person in the control system

You are trusting them to do the job, and trusting them with the authority to make decisions. Trust them to work with you to develop an effective control system that will ensure that the job will be completed successfully. The key task here is really to decide, ideally together, on effective checkpoints in order to:

■ monitor (and, if need be, influence) progress to ensure that the various stages, and the overall results that you need, are achieved on time and to the right standards.

■ discuss/review any major decisions to ensure that the criteria have been adequately met.

■ reassure the person who is doing the task that things are progressing as they should.

IDENTIFYING WHAT *SHOULD* HAPPEN

This is a joint activity between the manager and the delegatee. The manager knows the overall objective, i.e. the result expected. Assuming that the delegatee accepts this as realistic, he or she would usually suggest HOW they would go about achieving that result, together with any deadlines. If they only have experience of similar tasks they may need some guidance on standards/criteria, but try asking for their views first.

A key principle here is to encourage the delegatee to suggest when you should both meet to review progress.

They will usually identify exactly the same checkpoints that you would propose, and it eliminates the need for you to go over to their desk and play 'Long John Silver's parrot'! There is also likely to be more ownership to their plan than the manager's plan. They have suggested the checkpoints so they are likely to feel a personal responsibility to 'make it happen' by the deadlines.

MONITORING WHAT IS *ACTUALLY* HAPPENING

This should be a 'coal- face' activity. The person closest to the action is the one who can best monitor what is going on, *in time to act*. In a game, it is the players who have to make instant decisions. There is usually plenty of advice from the crowd but they aren't running with the ball! In delegation, monitoring can be done quite effectively enough by the delegatee, providing that they understand, and are committed to, the need to do it. They need to be involved in the process of identifying what to measure, and how to measure it.

Asking them what they would measure and how is usually the best way. It sounds obvious, but the irony is that few managers actually DO this.

IDENTIFYING ANY SIGNIFICANT VARIATION

Again, this is best done by the delegatee. All they need to know is the meaning of 'significant' variation. As we have mentioned before, the manager may well need to delegate authority to make independent decisions. This should include limits to help them to identify any potentially *significant* variations. Two examples might illustrate this.

Cash limits

The manager might delegate the task of buying a new computer to a team member, setting purchase cost limits of £1500 +/– 10%. The delegatee then knows that anything over £1650 or under £1350 would represent a significant variation. If the best choice fell outside this range, the team member would need to discuss the situation with the manager before ordering.

167

Time limits

A manager delegates the preparation of a departmental report for a meeting next Friday, and agrees to review the findings with a team member at 3pm on Thursday. The team member knows that however they plan their time, they must have everything ready for the meeting with the manager on Thursday. Any event that might adversely affect meeting that deadline would constitute a significant variation and would need to be discussed immediately with the manager.

PROMPT THE NEED FOR TIMELY CORRECTIVE ACTION

If problems have occurred before, e.g. deadlines have been missed, it is worth discussing what actions should be taken by the delegatee (or the manager) to, ideally, prevent the problem or, at least, handle it effectively if it arises.

By agreeing the control system with the delegatee, they will monitor what is going on and, because they are 'at the coal-face' should be able to take timely action before things go too far.

It might be useful at this point to provide an example to illustrate the benefits of developing the control system together and then delegating the control.

This story concerns a secretary in a training department. Courses covering a vast range of topics/skills were run in a purpose-built training centre and the trainees were given rooms in the residential centre as well. Course rooms and trainee accommodation were booked by at least five separate departments, so there was the potential for administrative slips-ups (omissions or double bookings). Some of you might say, *'Hang on, a good system should really prevent this.'* We agree but the best laid plans of mice and men, etc. . . With the best will in the world you cannot be certain of preventing everything. What would you say if the managing director says to you, *'I need four large training rooms for a company meeting next week. Sorry about the short notice but it is vital we hold it there and on that day.'*?

One of the training managers gave his secretary the task of monitoring these 'bookings' to ensure that all of the courses took place as planned; something for which the manager was responsible (and accountable). They discussed what should happen in the event of a problem, e.g. discovering a double-booking, and agreed that the course (and the trainees) should be moved to a local hotel. They then decided on a sensible budget, having checked with several local hotels who were pleased about the potential business, even at short notice.

The first time that this situation arose was when the manager was on holiday. The problem arose on the Friday morning for a course commencing on the following Monday. Due to the previous discussions, the secretary handled it immediately without the need to refer to anyone for approval. She contacted the selected hotels, decided which could best meet those particular requirements and made all of the arrangements within an hour. If she had needed to discuss what should happen, contact possible venues, get approval, then actually make the arrangements, it is highly unlikely that the course would have taken place. As it was, the trainees arrived at the training centre on Sunday night and were simply redirected to the hotel one mile away, where everything was ready and waiting for them.

168

The follow-up meeting; its importance and how to run it

On the surface, the follow-up meeting does not really seem to be a part of the 'control system' because it takes place after the event. It is the final step in the control process. Now that the task has been completed, the final outcome is reviewed against the objective, and the delegatee's performance throughout the task is discussed to identify strengths and areas for future improvement are identified.

WHY IS FOLLOW-UP IMPORTANT?

People like to know how they have done!

Very often, if the task was performed successfully, the manager just says 'thanks' and that is that. It's a shame if that is *all* that happens, because a discussion after the event can yield so much more. Some people seem to have an operating philosophy that says, 'If things are going wrong, I will discuss it with you. If things are going well, I will leave you alone'. If the job has gone well, 'leaving them alone' does not help to establish WHY it went well, and the opportunity to reinforce those strengths is also lost. Not only can you say 'thanks', you can build on their strengths, identify what has been learned, and agree any areas for future improvement.

HOW TO HANDLE THE FOLLOW-UP DISCUSSION

There is a close parallel with an appraisal discussion. If you are involved with appraisals, the structure is very similar. The key difference is that you are discussing performance on a single task, rather than someone's overall performance over a six- or twelve-month period. If you are not involved with appraisals, don't worry. We will outline what is involved in this meeting.

The duration of this meeting will depend on the complexity of the delegated task, and their performance of it. You would not really want to spend one and a half hours reviewing a fifteen-minute routine task. Having said that, a brief word of thanks can go a long way! The ideas that follow relate to reviewing performance on the more significant delegated tasks.

Preparation

Preparation for this meeting is just as important as when delegating the task originally. Firstly, think about why you asked them to do that particular task, and whether your objective for them has been achieved. Consider their performance of the task, i.e. was the task objective met or exceeded?, etc. Then look at what they did well and why, and what they could improve and how. Again, you might ask them to do some preparation prior to the meeting.

A suggested structure for the follow-up discussion

The basic principle is to *involve them as much as possible*.

■ Put the person at ease, explain the purpose of the discussion (to review performance on the task they have completed), and agree the objective for the meeting.

169

■ Review the objective for the task.

Ask them:

■ how they felt that it went, and what result they think was achieved?

■ what went well, and why they think that was?

■ what could have been improved, and how that might be done?

Add your own views, by all means, but try to get most of the information from them,

■ Decide on an action plan with dates, to reinforce the strengths, and address any areas for improvement.

■ If it has not already been covered, find out what they feel that they gained from doing the task, and explain what you gained from their help with the task.

■ Summarise the key points, and thank them.

170

SUMMARY – CHAPTER 10

■ 'Control' is monitoring the preformance of a delegated task so that the expected results are successfully achieved.

■ A 'control system' needs to:
  – identify what SHOULD happen,
  – monitor what is ACTUALLY happening,
  – identify any SIGNIFICANT VARIATION,
  – and prompt TIMELY, CORRECTIVE action, aimed at the cause.

■ Ensure that the control system is not just a management history book.

■ The best control systems are often SIMPLE!

■ *Involve the delegatee in the whole control process* in order to avoid perceived management 'interference'.
  Consider the KEY activities and identify the checkpoints.
  If you are delegating authority, setting limits will help them to identify any potentially significant variations.
  Encourage them to identify when you should meet to review progress. (This is a key point!)

■ Trust them to operate as much of the control system as possible.

■ The follow-up meeting is important! It 'closes the loop'. The discussion should cover what went well and why, and what could have been improved, and how.

11

Handling difficulties

Overview of this chapter

Unfortunately, despite good preparation and briefing, not all delegated tasks run perfectly. Little 'gremlins' have been known to creep in and disrupt things. This chapter concentrates on what you can do if difficulties occur 'along the way'.

What are the objectives for this chapter?

When you have read this chapter, you should:

■ know how to recognise that there are difficulties
■ know how to discuss and effectively resolve the issues
■ know when to 'call a halt'.

What is covered in this chapter?

■ Recognising the signs.
■ Discussing the difficulties.
■ The power of good questioning.
■ Providing advice or guidance.
■ Knowing when to 'call a halt'

Recognising the signs

The most obvious 'sign' is that the person to whom you delegated the task uses the 'lifeline' and asks to discuss difficulties with you. In this case, all you need do is respond to their request.

Secondly, the control system that you have jointly agreed should provide a clear indication that things are going wrong. For example, deadlines being missed or failure to meet the quality standards.

However, there is another equally important sign but one that is much harder to define – 'feelings'. In day-to-day discussions (not necessarily anything to do with the task) with the person concerned, you might get the 'feeling' that all is not well, even though they have not expressed any concern, and no deadline has been missed (yet).

'LIFELINE' SIGNS

During the delegation discussion, you said something like, 'If you have any concerns as the job progresses, just come in and talk'. So, part way through the task, they do just that. All you need to do is to make the time and respond to it! You may not be able to do it at that precise moment but fix a specific time (and put it in your diary), rather than say that you will see them later. Do not ignore this use of the 'lifeline' by them even though the person might just need some reassurance. If you have told them to use it, you must be prepared to play your part. Side-stepping the discussion is likely to make them feel that you said it but didn't really mean it, so they won't bother again.

'CONTROL SYSTEM' SIGNS

During the original delegation discussion, you and the delegatee jointly decided how best to control the task, set up checkpoints (deadlines/reviews) and agreed quality standards. Signs of difficulty would include:

- unreasonable excuses for failure to meet an agreed deadline
- reticence to attend the review discussion(s)
- performance below the level you would expect from that person, considering their skills, knowledge, and previous experience. For example, ignoring or failing to meet a quality standard that you have both agreed is realistic.

When these situations arise, you may have to instigate the discussion. They have not used the 'lifeline'. Why?

'FEELINGS' SIGNS

This is a difficult 'sign' to actually quantify. All we can really say here is that if you *feel* something is wrong or they are having difficulties, it is worth investigating (gently). Please try not to confuse this with any natural concern *you* may have about the result because you are accountable; they may be quite happy.

Explaining how you actually feel can be quite powerful. You would need to put this into your own words but we would suggest something like, 'Alan, I just get the feeling that you might have a concern about this part of the job. I've nothing concrete to go on so I could be totally wrong, but is there anything you want to discuss?' If they say 'No' you will have to leave it. Your feeling might indeed have been wrong. Alternatively, there is something wrong but they are not prepared to discuss it. In this case, you will need to wait until something more concrete emerges, probably via the control system.

Discussing the difficulties

At this point, you or they have recognised that there are problems with the task and you are about to sit down and try to resolve them together.

PREPARE, IF AT ALL POSSIBLE

173

Preparation is just as valuable here as it was for the original discussion. Depending on the situation, you may not have time, or any need, to prepare. For example, the issue may need immediate action or the difficulty is fairly simple to resolve.

If you have the opportunity to prepare

Decide your objective for the discussion; the person's skills and knowledge and their performance to date on the task; identify possible reasons for the difficulties and consider possible actions. The reason we have used 'possible' twice is that the actual discussion may uncover reasons/difficulties that you did not even know about, and the delegatee may be able to suggest actions themselves.

No opportunity to prepare

Decide your objective for the discussion as early as possible in the discussion so that you know clearly the result you need. Please remember that your objective identifies the outcome, not the method. For example, a way of resolving the difficulty has been found, rather than what that specific 'way' should be. This leaves the options open to input and suggestions from the delegatee.

THE DISCUSSION ITSELF

In this section, we will cover some general points relating to this type of discussion and suggest a broad structure that can help you to keep it 'on track'.

Putting the person at ease

The opening part of the discussion is important. Try to avoid a situation whereby the delegatee feels intimidated. Remember the discussion is not a 'witch-hunt'!

It is very important right at the start to help the person to understand that the whole purpose is to decide what can be done to resolve the difficulties. It will help to explain your intended approach, i.e. to discuss the difficulties and reasons for them, jointly decide what can be done to resolve them, and finally what is needed in order to complete the task.

Basically your approach needs to be positive ('We can resolve this'), and supportive ('We will identify the answers together'). This will encourage involvement that should then lead to commitment.

This is particularly important here as the person may feel that, because they are having difficulties, they are letting both you and themselves down. So they are likely to be feeling concerned. Secondly, *you* may be feeling concerned as well because, at the end of the day, you are accountable for the final result. Consequently, you may not be FEELING very positive and supportive. (Hopefully, the difficulties have been recognised in time to do something about them, so all should not be lost.)

174

A broad structure for the discussion

It is only possible to indicate a 'broad' structure here as the 'track' of the discussion will depend very much on information and ideas coming back from the delegatee.

What do you feel are the main 'steps' or areas to cover in a discussion on delegation difficulties?

_____

_____

_____

_____

The basic principle is to *involve the delegatee as much as possible*. They need to 'own' the action plan and are more likely to be committed to one that they have developed, or helped to develop.

BROAD STRUCTURE FOR THE DISCUSSION

- Put them at ease; explain purpose and approach.
- Agree the objective for the discussion.
- Review what has already gone well, and why.
- Ask the delegatee to explain the difficulties, and the reasons.
- Ask for their ideas as to ways of overcoming them, (unless you know that they are totally 'stuck', or do not have the experience necessary to answer that question).
- Offer guidance/advice *only if appropriate*.
- Jointly agree an action plan to handle the difficulties.
- Decide what actions are now necessary to complete the task successfully.
- Summarise the key actions/deadlines.
- Check how the delegatee now feels.
- If the original review date is now inappropriate, agree a new data for a follow-up meeting.

175

You will have seen some parallels with the original delegation briefing but there are three aspects of this type of discussion that are worth elaborating:

- the power of good questioning
- providing advice or guidance
- knowing when to 'call a halt'.

The power of good questioning

In Chapter 8 'Handling the Discussion' we covered the importance of effective questions and suggested types of useful questions and how they might be used when delegating. Whilst the discussion regarding difficulties that we are covering in this chapter is different, those questions are still useful.

As a brief reminder, they are:

- Open – to collect fairly general information and opinions.
- Probing – to get down to specifics.

- Clarifying – to ensure understanding.
- Closed – to confirm or deny (These have limited use).

There are two other types of question that can be particularly useful (or necessary) in a discussion on difficulties:

- Reflective.
- Confronting.

THE REFLECTIVE QUESTION

This question 'reflects back' what someone has said and encourages them to go further. An example of this might be . . .

Delegatee: *'I'm having some problems with those overhead transparencies for the presentation.'*
Manager: *'Problems with the transparencies?'*
Delegatee: *'Well, yes. I'm not at all sure about the amount of detail to include, or even how many to use for a 15-minute presentation'.*

A reflective question seems to act as a more gentle form of 'probe' question, and that may be very important when a person is feeling embarrassed or awkward.

THE CONFRONTING QUESTION

This question highlights an inconsistency between what is stated, and the facts.

Manager: *'How do you feel things are going, Mike?'*
Mike (the delegatee): *' No problems at all. Everything is going fine.'*
Manager: *'You said that there are no problems at all but didn't the Sales Department reject your draft proposal, Mike?'*

This type of question is extremely useful if the person does not accept that something is wrong (or will not admit to it!). It shows that there is a concern that needs to be resolved.

To 'confront' is defined as 'to face boldly'. It is important to make it clear that a 'confronting' question is *not* aggressive, i.e. an emotional attack. For example, an emotional attack would be something like, 'Don't lie to me, Mike. Are you daft enough to believe that I don't know that the Sales Department threw that proposal out?'

TWO QUESTIONS TO AVOID

In addition to the emotional attack above, there are two others to avoid:

- the leading question
- the loaded question.

The leading question

This one prompts the answer that the *questioner* wants. For example, 'There are two options to help you deal with this difficulty; on-job training or off-job training. I favour off-job training. Do you agree with that?' What is he or she supposed to reply, for goodness sake? They have already been told the answer! Sometimes, it is well meant; the manager is probably trying to help. However, it does not give the delegatee the chance of identifying the best answer for themselves.

The loaded question

This one appears similar but is very different. To us, the distinction is that the loaded question has unpleasant undertones. Very often these 'undertones' relate to fear.

For example, 'If you want to be a manager in this organisation, you will be able to handle the pressure involved in getting this task back on track, won't you?' So he or she is thinking, I can't say 'no'. If I do, my chances of a management job have gone out of the window because he will think I can't cope with pressure. As we have said before, trying to 'motivate' by fear is dangerous. Suppose they grudgingly say 'yes' the pressure is too much, and the task is a failure. If that delegatee were you, how would you view that manager (and delegation opportunities) in future?

Providing advice or guidance

Many people appear to equate giving help on difficulties with providing advice. When someone is having difficulties, giving advice may not be the answer! You may now be thinking, *Hang on though. I am supposed to give them a 'lifeline' right? Now you're saying that when they use it, I'm not to give them any advice.* Whilst there is a place for advice, it should not usually be the first action by the manager when people are having problems with a delegated task. Giving advice might answer the immediate issue, but it is often far more effective to

177

help them develop their own solution to the problem(s). This approach takes longer admittedly, but it will result in ownership of the plan and should teach them something about how to handle such problems in the future.

A colleague of ours used to say, 'Give someone a fish and you feed them for a day. Teach them to fish, and you feed them for life'. There is a lot of truth in that!

SO WHEN IS ADVICE APPROPRIATE?

In an earlier paragraph, we said that advice would not usually be the first action. If the difficulty has a simple solution, i.e. the person doesn't know where to find the instructions for something or other, of course, tell them the answer. Trying to involve them would yield nothing; they can't answer the questions! Involvement would probably irritate. Similarly, the difficulty may not be simple but, because of inexperience, they may not be able to work out the answers so advice is fine.

178

> **Give advice *only* when there is no *better* option!**

Generally, we believe that providing guidance is a better option than giving advice. 'Guidance' is helping them to develop their own solutions.

HOW DO YOU ACTUALLY PROVIDE THIS GUIDANCE?

By effective questioning! Good questions will help *them* to explore the difficulty that they are having, identify the cause(s), and develop solutions with your help. There are three questions that we have used in this situation time and time again:

- Tell me a bit more about that difficulty? (explores the difficulty).
- What do you think is causing that? (identifies the causes).
- What do you think we can do about that? (generates possible solutions).

By the way, please try to avoid using the word 'problem' if you can. It seems to be a fairly emotive word, i.e. people don't seem to mind having 'difficulties' but some don't like it much when told they are 'having problems'. 'Problems? I certainly haven't got any problems! What are you implying?'

What if they genuinely can't identify possible solutions to the difficulties?

Rather than advise too readily, try to outline some options for them, then encourage them to select the most suitable. For example:

John (delegatee): *'I'm not sure about the best approach, the style I suppose, to use for this talk to the team.'*
Shirley (manager): *'Have you got any ideas at all, John?'*
John: *'To be honest, I haven't a clue. As you know, I've never given a talk before'.*
Shirley: *'Well, there are two main options really: a fairly formal approach with visual aids, or a more light-hearted one that could include a bit of humour and examples from your own experiences. Which do you think would suit you and the topic best?'*

This approach leaves the choice to them (ownership again!).

179

Knowing when to 'call a halt'

Disaster strikes! This is something that every manager dreads. It is the stuff that nightmares are made of, causing us to wake up in a cold sweat, biting lumps out of the bedpost. Part way through the task something goes horribly wrong and you decide that there are only two options; step in and direct it, or withdraw the task and handle it yourself.

It is important to know **when** to actually 'call a halt'; and **how** to do it, with minimum damage to the person's feelings and the task. This situation is one that would cause concern to the most experienced managers. There is no easy answer, but it is important that you handle it in a way that suits you. What follows are some guidelines in which we believe. You will have to decide whether you agree with them and probably have to tailor those you like to suit your own approach. Before you reject any though, consider the alternative, and ask yourself which will work best for you. We can't guide you on that.

WHEN TO 'CALL A HALT'

When a major disaster is imminent (or is actually happening in front of you), and the important task will be a total failure unless you take personal control, by either directing it or doing it personally. (The control system should have shown up this potential disaster in time to correct matters, but the best laid plans . . .)

In this situation, do not delay the fateful moment! You aren't going to enjoy doing it and neither will the poor old delegatee, but that is no excuse for delay. If you are lucky, the potential disaster will become apparent when you are both talking in private. Life is not always so kind; occasionally you are faced with trying to handle a very 'public' disaster. The following example, whilst not strictly delegation in the normal sense, might illustrate some of the issues.

Some years ago, an organisation asked me to give one of their new trainers some up-front training experience (and coaching) on one of my courses, and I agreed. The new trainer (we will call him Jack) was very keen and knowledgeable about the topic of the session he had pre-prepared. We jointly decided that he would 'sit-in' on day one to get the feel of the course and then run his prepared session on day two. The group were extremely positive throughout day one and really stretched me with a lot of tough, but very valid questions. Quite a number of the questions were either exploring an issue in more depth, or healthy disagreement. (As you know, there are very few 'absolutes' in management). Anyway, that evening, Jack and I talked about the course, the group, and discussed his session on the coming day. Jack was concerned about how the group might react to him (after a day with me) and suggested going on first, so a new day started with him. He was also unsure whether he would be able to handle them with his limited experience. (I think he felt that he would be like Ben Hur during the chariot race!) We spent a long time talking about how he might handle potential difficulties or tough questions and he asked for a brief session of tough questioning from me. I threw him the worst I could dream up and he coped very well.

The following morning before we started, he said he was still worried. I reassured him as best I could by saying that any trainer should be a bit nervous before a session. As you know, you can only support; you can't do it for them. At some point the person has to stand on their own feet and do it alone. I gave him the choice of running as we had planned, or delaying the session until later in the week to give him more time to prepare. Jack opted to run as planned.

He gave a superb introduction and the first fifteen minutes of his session was excellent. Then it started! The group got into their stride and threw the usual barrage of questions and, unfortunately, Jack couldn't cope. He answered a couple very well but then got totally confused and lost his way. He turned to me, with a really pained expression on his face, and said *'Sorry, John. I can't do this?'* The group immediately realised what they had done, apologised to him, and backed off rapidly. They liked him! I immediately called a coffee break so that Jack and I could sort it out.

To cut a long story short, I decided to take the rest of the session because it was the foundation for the rest of the work that followed. I spent a good proportion of that day wondering about how Jack must be feeling; I certainly felt badly about taking it away from him, but it had to be done.

Later in the week, Jack recovered his confidence. He was able to prepare and run an excellent training session with the group (who, on his instruction, were told to question as much as they wished – and they did!). So it all turned out right in the end.

In fairness, you might say that I should have made the decision earlier (the previous evening), you could be right but I believed that Jack *would* cope. I was accountable (my course!); the error in judgement was mine.

HOW TO HANDLE 'CALLING A HALT'

Stopping it isn't hard usually; doing it effectively and handling the feelings IS hard. What follows is based on the premise that they tried their best, it has all gone wrong for them, and you can personally handle the 'disaster' in some way.

Being realistic, this situation is bound to generate adverse feelings on both sides. They will feel that they have failed and will be embarrassed or even angry with themselves about it. You know that you have to stop it to avoid things getting any worse.

Deal with it privately, if you can

This will, at least, prevent the intense embarrassment generated by a 'public' stoppage of the type illustrated by our example.

If time is very short, i.e. crisis conditions, the first priority is to quickly review the situation and then decide what action is to be taken to avoid disaster, or minimise it. Having done that, arrange a further discussion. As soon as possible after the situation has been handled, objectively review what has happened, and why it has occurred. Try to jointly agree whether the person is capable of actually handling some future similar task. If so, jointly prepare a new action plan with them, ensuring that the cause of the disaster is properly addressed. Ensure that the person feels that it will adequately prevent any future disaster.

Without trying to be an amateur psychologist, try to help the person see the situation in as positive a light as possible. This might sound strange but if, for instance, it is the only disaster they have had in ten years they can't be doing too badly. It has happened, nothing can change that. Help them learn from it so that it does not recur. That should help to avoid a totally negative outcome to the discussion.

If you both decide that this sort of task is beyond them at the moment (an impossibility rather than a challenge) try to identify some other task on which you are fairly certain that they *will* succeed. If at all possible, try to get this task underway as soon as the person is ready to give it a try.

If you do conclude that this sort of task is an impossibility for them, you need to ask yourself why you selected this person for it in the first place? Was the disaster just plain bad luck, could it have been foreseen, or did it arise through some misjudgement of your own? You may feel that it was your fault. If so, as we have said before, it is important to actually say so. We believe that, generally, a person's respect for a manager goes up, not down, when that manager has the courage to admit they were wrong, once in a while. We all make mistakes; some people just never seem prepared to admit them.

If you are fortunate enough to have ample time, then all of the above points can be incorporated in the same discussion.

Consider the next step

In our example, Jack and I were able to resurrect matters, and he had the opportunity to try again quickly. This may not always be possible, of course. If, for example, someone makes a total mess of a departmental meeting and they want to try again, it may be three months before another opportunity is available.

The time lag seems less important than knowing that the opportunity will actually be there for them. After a disaster, there is a natural concern about whether they will ever be given a delegated task again. In your discussion with them, if you have used the guidelines, you will hopefully have identified an action plan for a future task. That task will either re-run the 'problem' task having dealt with the cause of the disaster, or it will be a simpler task. Try to ensure that the plan includes dates so that the person knows it will happen.

However, there is one other aspect to consider. If the delegatee asks for a bit of 'recovery' time before tackling something else, then, fair enough. The only caution is 'don't let it go on too long!' Some time ago, I fell off a horse when going over a very small jump, but was pretty shaken. My instructor (bless her) INSISTED that I 'get back on or you'll never ride again!' I did, ... and I did!

I think that the same principle applies here. Just ensure that, next time, they succeed!

SUMMARY – CHAPTER 11

- Recognising the signs:
  - don't ignore their use of the 'lifeline'.
  - unreasonable excuses for failure to meet deadlines.
  - reticence to attend review discussions.
  - performance below the level you would expect from that person.
  - if you feel that something is wrong, but check gently!
- Preparing to discuss the difficulties:
  - make time to prepare, if at all possible.
  - no time to prepare, set a clear objective right at the start.
- Handling the discussion about difficulties:
  - your approach should be positive (can resolve the difficulties) and supportive (identify the answers together).
  - recognise, and handle adverse feelings.
- Broad structure for the discussion:
  - agree objective for the discussion.
  - review what has already gone well, and why.
  - ask delegatee to explain difficulties and reasons.
  - where possible, ask for their ideas to overcome them.
  - generally, offer *guidance* (via questions), rather than advice.
  - jointly agree an action plan to handle the difficulties.
  - summarise, and check how delegatee feels.
  - arrange a review date.
- Questions:
  - open, probe clarify, closed (sparingly) as before
  - plus *reflecive* and *confronting*
  - avoid loaded or leading questions!
- Knowing when to 'call a halt':
  when a major disaster is imminent or acutally happening in front of you and the important task will be a total failure unless you take personal control.
  Don't delay action!
- How to 'call a halt':
  - *privately*, if at all possible, to avoid 'public' embarrassment.
  - if time is short, decide how best to handle the disaster, but arrange to have a later discussion.
  - *as soon as possible after the event*, review what happened and why, try to help them learn from it to make it as positive as possible, and decide on what happens next (another try, or a different task).
    Try to help them leave the discussion with as positive an outcome as possible, so that they do not feel that all has been lost.

183

12

Pulling it all together

Overview of this chapter

Well, you have done it! This last chapter is really a review. We have tried to show you HOW you can 'Let Go Without Losing Control', so, by now, we hope that you have gained some ideas to help. We have also included an activity so that you can compare your knowledge and approach NOW with that which you employed right at the start of the book. This should help you, in the last section, to identify what you have gained from reading this book.

What are the objectives for this chapter?

When you have read this chapter, you should:

■ have reviewed the key points covered in this book

■ have compared your views on or approach to delegation NOW having read the book, with the views and approach you employed right at the start of the book.

■ have identified what you have learned from reading the book, and decided what, if anything, you will do differently in future. (We say 'if anything' because the book might have simply reinforced what you were already doing.)

What is covered in this chapter?

■ Key point outlines covering:
  – definition of delegation,
  – choosing the right task to delegate,
  – choosing the right (most suitable) person for the task,
  – preparing to delegate,
  – handling the delegation discussion,

- obtaining genuine commitment,
- control without interference,
- handling difficulties.

■ How would you 'Let go without losing control' NOW: an activity to enable you to compare your views and approach now with those at the start of the book.

■ What have you learned from reading this book?

Key point outlines

WHAT IS DELEGATION?

Entrusting part of your job as a manager to someone else (usually a team member), together with the responsibility for its achievement and the authority necessary to carry it out.

CHOOSING THE RIGHT TASK TO DELEGATE – OBJECTIVE SETTING

■ Set the objective at the right level

An effective objective should:

■ be *result*-oriented, rather than activity-oriented

■ be clear, measurable (if possible), and realistic

■ show the result expected, the deadline and any constraints.

CHOOSING THE RIGHT TASK TO DELEGATE – DECIDING WHICH TASK

Those tasks which:

■ help you to make better use of your time

■ develop members of your team

■ help you motivate people in the team

■ enable 'better' decisions, by allowing you more time for your major decisions, and by using the abilities of your team.

Key points to remember:

■ 'What am I here for?'

■ Don't confuse 'urgent' with 'important'

▶

- Your 'routine' tasks can be interesting to others
- Avoid the 'Ostrich' approach – hoping the danger might go away
- Staff development is an important part of your job as a manager
- Delegate using the 'building block' approach
- Accept minor mistakes; they are inevitable, with delegated work
- Involve the person to help identify 'interesting work'
- Accept that some people in your team may do some things better than you. Be grateful for it!

CHOOSING THE RIGHT (MOST SUITABLE) PERSON FOR THE TASK

- Identify the skills and knowledge needed to successfully complete the delegated task, and rate them to show importance.
- Break the task down into 'key tasks' if it helps the analysis.
- Identify the skills and knowledge of people in our team, and rate them to show present level (or desired level).
- Use the format of the form in the chapter to record and update information.

187

The levels of delegation:

- **Level 1** – Do it with you, help with detail, frequent monitoring.
- **Level 2** – They do important things with you, the rest on their own with checkpoints set by you.
- **Level 3** – They decide what help they need and set the checkpoints. They may want to review major decisions with you prior to implementation.
- **Level 4** – Full delegation; review objective (including any constraints) with them. Let them go, advise you of decisions/outcome after the event.
- Two traps to avoid:
  - 'No experience means no ability'.
  - 'This will be a challenge for you.' (challenge versus impossibility)

PREPARING TO DELEGATE

- Review the objective – clear, measurable (if possible), realistic, shows result, deadline, and any constraints.

▶

- Consider the background – task, person, any skill or knowledge gaps.
- Review the level:

  level 1 – no experience

  level 2 – knows the basics

  level 3 – reasonable experience

  level 4 – fully experienced
- Decide the authority needed.
- Identify the control checkpoints (in case they miss any).
- If feasible, encourage/help them to prepare.
- Allow ample time for the discussion.

HANDLING THE DELEGATION DISCUSSION (GUIDELINES)

Starting the discussion off on the right foot:
- Put the person at ease
- If this is the first discussion, explain background: why task is needed, why that person, and purpose of discussion.

The main body of the discussion:
- Check that the task is feasible, i.e. check workload issues.
- Review skills and knowledge, and any gaps.
- Make their responsibilities clear, or help them to clarify them.
- Show confidence in them – praise, not flattery.
- Ask effective questions, mainly open, probing, and clarifying.
- Summarise whenever it helps both of you.
- Involve them to whatever extent their experience allows, and decide whether to allow/prevent minor mistakes.
- Jointly produce the plan, building on their ideas as much as possible.
- Discuss potential difficulties, and decide how to handle.
- Give them adequate authority.
- Discuss and agree the controls.
- Give them a 'lifeline'.

Ending the discussion effectively:
- Summarise the key actions and agreements.
- Check how the person actually feels about doing the task.
- Arrange a follow-up meeting to take place after the event.
- Close; remind them of the 'lifeline', and thank them.

OBTAINING GENUINE COMMITMENT

- 'Genuine commitment' is a willing, enthusiastic agreement to carry out the task to the best of that person's ability.

- Don't try for 'genuine commitment' when you can only realistically expect 'acceptance', e.g. boring task.

- How to obtain genuine commitment:
  - Ensure your expectations are realistic.
  - Involve them in the whole process.
  - Show that minor mistakes will be accepted.
  - Help to identify the benefits to *them* of carrying out the task.
  - If delegating to improve motivation, ensure that you *really* know what motivates that person.

- Realistic expectations:
  - Explain why you think they can handle the task.
  - Why you feel as you do (to explain things that you can't prove).
  - Resolve any concerns that they may have.

- Involve them in the whole process:
  - There seems to be a strong link between involvement and commitment.
  - Avoid 'pseudo-democracy', i.e. *pretending* to involve them.
  - Watch out for 'Smiling Lemmings'.
  - Be prepared to actually *back* their decisions!

- Helping to identify the benefits to *them* of doing the task:
  - If there are *no* benefits, don't try to invent them!
  - Ask *them* what they see as the benefits of doing the task.

- If delegating to improve motivation, ensure that you really know what motivates them:
  - Motivation should be positive (encouragement), rather than negative (fear).
  - Ask them 'What do you enjoy doing (at work), and why?'
  - Don't assume that you know the answers to the previous questions.
  - When choosing the task, ensure it is within their capabilities and provides the motivation factors you have jointly identified.
  - At the end of the discussion, check how they feel about doing the task.

- What if you don't get the commitment that you need?:
  Three options:
  - If you decide to stop it there, try to jointly arrive at the decision to abandon it, and show that it has not removed future opportunities.
  - You might decide that 'commitment' is unrealistic, and something slightly better than acceptance is adequate, i.e. when enthusiasm will only be generated after some of the work has been successfully completed.
  - Find out what went wrong, and try again. Identify the reasons for lack of commitment with their help, and involve them in identifying what can be done to resolve the concerns.

189

CONTROL WITHOUT INTERFERENCE

- 'Control' is monitoring the performance of a delegated task so that the expected results are successfully achieved.
- A 'control system' needs to:
  - identify what SHOULD happen,
  - monitor what is ACTUALLY happening,
  - identify any SIGNIFICANT VARIATION,
  - and prompt TIMELY, CORRECTIVE action, aimed at the cause.
- Ensure that the control system is not just a management history book.
- The best control systems are often SIMPLE!
- *Involve the delegatee in the whole control process* in order to avoid perceived management 'interference'.
  - Consider the KEY activities and identify the checkpoints.
  - If you are delegating authority, setting limits will help them to identify any potentially significant variations.
  - Encourage them to identify when you should meet to review progress. (This is a key point!)
- Trust them to operate as much of the control system as possible.
- The follow-up meeting is important!

  It 'closes the loop'. The discussion should cover what went well and why, and what could have been improved, and how.

HANDLING DIFFICULTIES

- Recognising the signs:
  - don't ignore their use of the 'lifeline'.
  - unreasonable excuses for failure to meet deadlines.
  - reticence to attend review discussions.
  - performance below the level you would expect from that person.
  - if you feel that something is wrong, but check gently!
- Preparing to discuss the difficulties:
  - make time to prepare, if at all possible.
  - no time to prepare, set a clear objective right at the start.
- Handling the discussion about difficulties:
  - your approach should be positive (can resolve the difficulties).
  - and supportive (identify the answers together).
  - recognise, and handle adverse feelings.

- Broad structure for the discussion:
  - agree objective for the discussion.
  - review what has already gone well, and why.
  - ask delegatee to explain difficulties and reasons.
  - where possible, ask for their ideas to overcome them.
  - generally, offer guidance (via questions), rather than advice.
  - jointly agree an action plan to handle the difficulties.
  - summarise, and check how delegatee feels.
  - arrange a review date.
- Questions:
  - open, probe clarify, closed (sparingly) as before.
  - plus reflective and confronting.
  - avoid loaded or leading questions!
- Knowing when to 'call a halt':
  - when a major disaster is imminent or actually happening in front of you and the important task will be a total failure unless you take personal control.
  - Don't delay action!
- How to 'call a halt':
  - privately, if at all possible, to avoid 'public' embarrassment.
  - if time is short, decide how best to handle the disaster, but arrange to have a later discussion.
  - as soon as possible after the event, review what happened and why, try to help them learn from it to make it as positive as possible, and decide on what happens next (another try, or a different task)
  - Try to help them leave the discussion, with as positive an outcome as possible, so that they do not feel that all has been lost.

191

How would you 'let go without losing control' *now*?

This activity will enable you to compare your approach to delegation having read this book, with the one you employed in the activity 'How good a delegator are you?' in Chapter 2. Read the situation that follows and decide how you, as the 'Conference Banqueting Manager', would handle it. We have purposely left this brief broad so that you can include any aspects that you consider to be important.

Note your ideas down in the section that follows the situation. After this, for comparison, we have again listed out the factors that we consider to be important here. You will then be able to identify how your approach differs from that used in the example in Chapter 2.

THE SITUATION

You are the Conference Banqueting Manager in a medium-sized catering firm, dealing with all types of catering functions. You have an Assistant Manager, two supervisors (and small teams), and, as the smallest of the two departments dealing with banqueting, are responsible solely for the large commercial conferences and functions (200 to 500 people). The other banqueting department deals with small in-company functions (up to 200 people) and private parties, of which there are many.

Yesterday you received a phone call from one of the Directors (Charles) who is a very keen cricketer and is very influential in the town, often sponsoring events (large and small) in aid of various charities. He explained that he had heard of an event sponsored by a local firm (of whom he is a shareholder) to raise money for a much-needed children's unit at the local hospital. The event is to be a fancy-dress cricket match between a guest team from Oxbridge University and the locals daft enough to take part. The match is in two weeks' time and the charity organisers have just been informed that the firm who were booked to provide the catering facilities have 'backed-out'. All the invitations and adverts have gone out and the guest team only fitted the match in to an already tight schedule because they knew it was for charity. Charles therefore stepped in to 'save the day' by agreeing to provide the necessary catering, at the same cost. This has left you with a dilemma – on the one hand you and your department could benefit long term if this was handled well (many potential customers will be there). However two weeks is not long! You discussed the function with your Assistant Manager and she explained that the only way that your department can possibly meet the commitment is to get additional help from the other banqueting department. The difficulty is that they will see little benefit from being asked to help with a function catering for 1000 people, apart from the fact that Charles will know they have helped.

The Managing Director has just told you that you must leave for an important business trip abroad in two days time (to advise a subsidiary of a major client) and you will not return until after the cricket match. Under normal circumstances, you would personally request co-operation from another department when required, but, as the people concerned are absent at the moment, you will need to delegate the task to your Assistant Manager, Penny. She is very experienced in managing catering arrangements of this size and type of function (and was totally comfortable when you discussed it with her yesterday providing that extra help is obtained), is an excellent 'people-manager', but has limited inter-departmental 'selling' experience (three previous occasions with the Finance Dept.). Penny has successfully acted as 'stand-in' for you in the past and has made several informal presentations, but might lack some confidence in handling this particular situation.

Penny will need to convince the Area Supervisor (Carlos) in the other banqueting department to provide four staff (out of total of 20) to help prepare for and serve at the cricket match. One year ago Carlos applied for the position that Penny now holds, but was turned down due to her far greater catering experience. There was an initial period of minor resentment, compounded by the fact that the job of Assistant Manager is one grade higher than that of Area Supervisor and consequently pays more. Carlos and Penny now seem to have a reasonable working relationship. Both Carlos and his manager are currently attending a catering conference and Carlos will not return to the office for three days. His manager will be there for a further four days as a 'speaker'.

193

How would you delegate the task to Penny of obtaining co-operation (and four staff) from Carlos?

Note: For the purposes of this exercise, you do not need to discuss Penny's actual management of the charity function.

Before the discussion:

_____

_____

_____

_____

_____

_____

_____

_____

_____

_____

_____

During the discussion:

_____

_____

_____

_____

_____

_____

_____

_____

_____

_____

_____

_____

_____

After the discussion:

_____

_____

_____

_____

_____

_____

_____

_____

_____

_____

_____

_____

_____

_____

THE FACTORS THAT WE CONSIDER TO BE IMPORTANT

Before the discussion

Objective Decide the result that you expect Penny to achieve, i.e. obtain the loan of four staff from Carlos' team to help prepare for and serve at the forthcoming cricket match in two weeks time.
(Note: the objective you set should not have anything to do with the actual management of the cricket function itself; this is NOT a delegated task, she does this anyway.)

Background Why Penny is selected, why the task is important and must be delegated, why additional help is needed from Carlos' team, Director's interest in the project, benefits of doing this project. Consider how Penny might feel about asking Carlos for help.

Talk to Charles Check the budget with him, authority for Penny, and discuss his involvement in the event of outright refusal by Carlos to help. (Note: you may have handled this differently. Ask yourself if your approach would succeed. If so, fine!)

Note to Carlos and Manager Brief note just to say that Penny is standing-in during your absence.

Experience Although Penny is an experienced Assistant Manager, the delegated task involves inter-departmental 'selling' in which she has reasonable experience, so we would put her at level 3. (You should not have fallen into the trap of putting her at level 4. She is not 'fully experienced and comfortable' with inter-departmental 'selling'!). Penny's strengths are people skills, working knowledge, successfully acting as 'stand-in'. 'Weakness' is that she may lack the confidence to assertively persuade Carlos because of the background.

Authority What authority might Penny need? What if Carlos refuses to help?

Checkpoints Is a discussion likely to be needed with Penny (or Charles, even) before you leave?

During the discussion

Remember from the brief and objective that you do not need to discuss Penny's actual management of the cricket function; that has not been delegated!

You need to show trust and confidence in Penny throughout the discussion. Remember that she can cope adequately with the 'mechanics' of doing such a task (three previous discussions with Finance); the problem will be having the confidence to persuade Carlos.

Opening Put at ease, review the background and benefits, why Carlos has to be convinced, why the task of convincing him is being delegated to Penny (and watch her reaction closely), establish the benefits that Penny might see (when she has got over the shock!), and the purpose of this discussion.

Main body:

Feasibility Review Penny's current commitments. Is it feasible for her to see Carlos on his return in three days? (Did you consider any contingency plan in case it was impossible for her to see him in time?)

Review her skills and knowledge Full involvement is needed here. Ask for her view of strengths and weaknesses. Ensure that she knows how her strengths will help here. Build confidence by factual examples, i.e. three previous successful discussions with Finance. Her concern is likely to be around confidence, not ability. What help does she need from you (within two days) to alleviate any concerns?

Make responsibilities clear Agree the specific objective for the discussion with Penny, i.e. obtain the loan of four staff from Carlos' team to help prepare for and serve at the forthcoming cricket match in two weeks time. At this point, you could explain the budget for the project or you could leave that until the 'authority' section later.

Show confidence in them We mentioned this at the start but, as a quick reminder, remember that praise is very different from flattery. Praise, based on fact, will help to build confidence.

Questions Penny has reasonable experience (level 3) so open and probe questions can be extensively used to obtain her views and ideas. Remember to clarify to ensure joint understanding.

Jointly produce the plan Commitment is important here so involve Penny by getting her to decide the steps necessary to prepare for and run the discussion with Carlos when he returns. Pay particular attention to any 'steps' that help her confidence.

Discuss potential difficulties Again, ask Penny to identify any, and suggest appropriate actions. Those we highlighted are:

(a) Carlos sees Penny as simply 'pulling rank' whilst the bosses are away and reacts adversely. Action: careful positioning and explanation of why situation has arisen. Request co-operation and involve Carlos as much as possible. (Penny should not push for enthusiastic commitment from Carlos when acceptance would probably be sufficient.)

(b) Outright refusal by Carlos to help. Action: Ask him to outline the consequences of refusal, i.e. try to change his mind. If all else fails, Penny to involve Charles (explain result of any prior conversation that you have had with Charles – see prep.). In this case, all Penny is likely to get is grudging acceptance by Carlos but that may be sufficient. It would not however do much to aid their future working relationship so should be avoided if at all possible.

Give adequate authority Penny may need authority to pay overtime within the budget. This would be particularly important for the 'loan' staff who would not normally be under her authority. Penny would not want to be unsure about what she could or couldn't do.

Discuss and agree controls These will stem from the plan, and should come from Penny (as you won't be there!) She may ask to see you before you leave to review any plan for handling Carlos that she might prepare over the next two days. Penny will need to know what action to take if Carlos gives her an outright refusal.

Give a 'lifeline' Access to you before you actually leave and a phone number if you can be contacted. Access to Charles during your absence if Penny chooses to use it.

Ending the discussion:

Summarise key actions and agreements Not much we can add here; just do it and ensure that everything is clear.

Check how the person actually feels Ensure that she feels sufficiently confident to handle Carlos.

Arrange a follow-up meeting This is vital to review how things went, and how the relationship with Carlos now stands.

Close the discussion Remind them of the 'lifelines' and thank them for agreeing to help.

After the discussion

'Lifeline' Ensure that you respond to any requests by Penny for help or guidance before you leave, (but don't interfere!).

Talk to Charles If anything significant (that might involve him) came out from your meeting with Penny.

Are there any *significant* differences between your list of factors and approach compared with ours?

Your list of factors or approach might have differed in some respects but that does not mean you were 'wrong'. Ask yourself whether your (different) approach would have produced the right result, for the right reasons. If the answer is 'yes', you were not wrong. Remember that we have said all along that **there is no one right way!**

If the answer to the question is 'no' then note below what you now think you should have done differently.

_____

_____

_____

_____

_____

_____

_____

_____

Finally, compare your approach to this situation with that you applied to the situation facing the Training Manager in Chapter 2. You might like to summarise the key differences in your approach here as they will help you with the final section of this chapter, 'What have you learned from reading this book?' that follows.

_____

_____

_____

_____

_____

_____

_____

_____

_____

What have you learned from reading this book?

Look back at the last section of Chapter 2 where you identified your strengths and weaknesses, together with the results you wanted from reading this book. Look through the notes you made on the Key Points section at the end of each chapter, and at your conclusions from the preceding activity.

What you will do (or try to do) differently when delegating?

_____

_____

_____

_____

_____

_____

199

_____

_____

_____

_____

_____

_____

_____

_____

_____

_____

_____

_____

_____

_____

Conclusion

The perfect delegator has yet to be 'built', and no book can achieve that for you. What we *do* hope is that you have gained some practical ideas on 'Letting Go Without Losing Control', as a result of reading this book and using the activities that we have included.

We also trust that you enjoyed reading it as much as we enjoyed writing it. Please do not see the ideas in here as written on tablets of stone. You will have to tailor them to suit your own approach, and decide when the idea applies to a particular situation. Remember that 'there is no one right way' in management, but we hope that you have gained some practical ideas to add to your 'management toolbox'!

If you find yourself working with us on one of our management skills courses at some future date, we look forward to meeting you and will enjoy talking to you about any issues raised in this book.

We wish you well for the future.

Index

201